A SHORTCUT TO
DRUNKARD'S PATH
Easy Appliqué Curves

Ann Frischkorn
and Amy Sandrin

Martingale®
& C O M P A N Y

CREDITS

President • Nancy J. Martin
CEO • Daniel J. Martin
VP and General Manager • Tom Wierzbicki
Publisher • Jane Hamada
Editorial Director • Mary V. Green
Managing Editor • Tina Cook
Technical Editor • Laurie Baker
Copy Editor • Sheila Chapman Ryan
Design Director • Stan Green
Illustrator • Laurel Strand
Cover Designer • Stan Green
Text Designer • Shelly Garrison
Photographer • Brent Kane

A Shortcut to Drunkard's Path: Easy Appliqué Curves
© 2005 by Ann Frischkorn and Amy Sandrin

That Patchwork Place® is an imprint of
Martingale & Company®.

Martingale & Company
20205 144th Avenue NE
Woodinville, WA 98072-8478 USA
www.martingale-pub.com

Printed in China

10 09 08 07 06 05   8 7 6 5 4 3 2 1

Library of Congress Cataloging-in-Publication Data
Frischkorn, Ann.
    A shortcut to Drunkard's Path : easy appliqué curves / Ann Frischkorn and Amy Sandrin.
        p. cm.
    ISBN 1-56477-598-4
    1. Patchwork—Patterns. 2. Quilting—Patterns. 3. Appliqué—Patterns. I. Sandrin, Amy. II. Title.
    TT835.F7555 2005
    746.46'041—dc22
                                    2004027880

MISSION STATEMENT
Dedicated to providing quality products
and service to inspire creativity.

DEDICATION

This book is dedicated to twins. It's an awesome feeling to have a sibling who is your best friend, your business partner, and most importantly, your twin. Each of us could go it alone, but together we are twice as creative, twice as inspired, and we have twice as much fun. Here's to twins all over the world.

ACKNOWLEDGMENTS

Special thanks to our family members. To our husbands, Dave and Don, for encouraging our obsessive passion for quilting. And to our kids, Anthony, Kyle, Eric, and Kate: thanks for making labels, trimming tons of circles, and never complaining about quick-and-easy meals.

Thanks to Terry Martin, Karen Soltys, Laurie Baker, and everyone at Martingale & Company for making the entire process as easy as a Sunday drive down a sunny country lane with the car top down.

CONTENTS

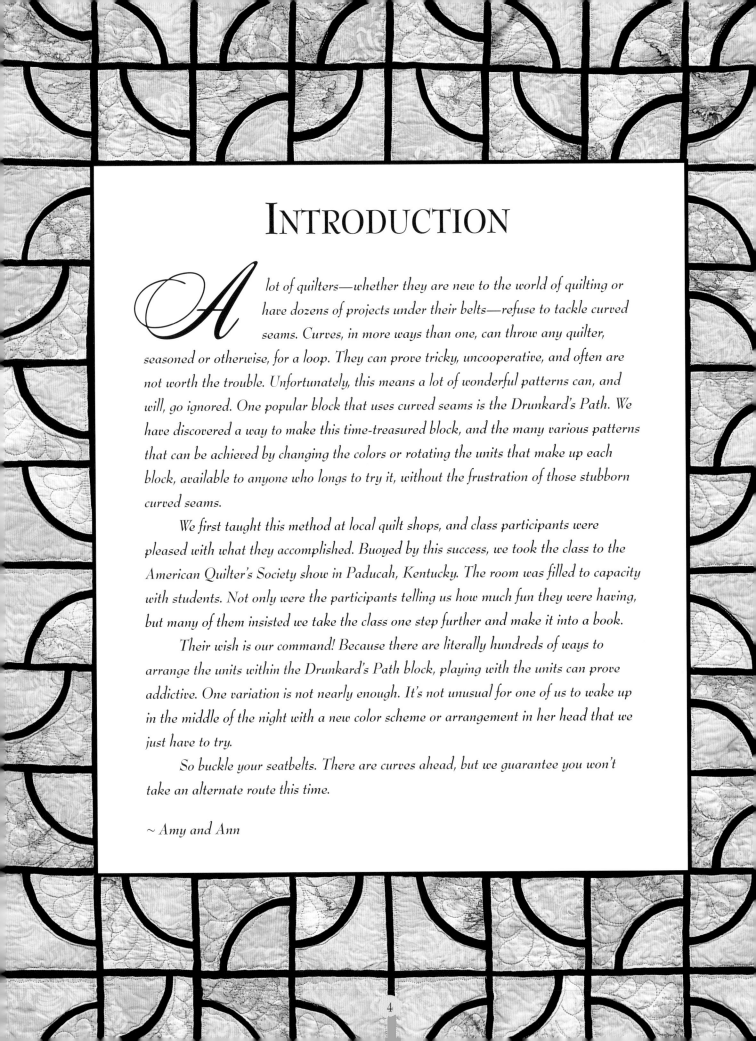

INTRODUCTION

A lot of quilters—whether they are new to the world of quilting or have dozens of projects under their belts—refuse to tackle curved seams. Curves, in more ways than one, can throw any quilter, seasoned or otherwise, for a loop. They can prove tricky, uncooperative, and often are not worth the trouble. Unfortunately, this means a lot of wonderful patterns can, and will, go ignored. One popular block that uses curved seams is the Drunkard's Path. We have discovered a way to make this time-treasured block, and the many various patterns that can be achieved by changing the colors or rotating the units that make up each block, available to anyone who longs to try it, without the frustration of those stubborn curved seams.

We first taught this method at local quilt shops, and class participants were pleased with what they accomplished. Buoyed by this success, we took the class to the American Quilter's Society show in Paducah, Kentucky. The room was filled to capacity with students. Not only were the participants telling us how much fun they were having, but many of them insisted we take the class one step further and make it into a book.

Their wish is our command! Because there are literally hundreds of ways to arrange the units within the Drunkard's Path block, playing with the units can prove addictive. One variation is not nearly enough. It's not unusual for one of us to wake up in the middle of the night with a new color scheme or arrangement in her head that we just have to try.

So buckle your seatbelts. There are curves ahead, but we guarantee you won't take an alternate route this time.

~ Amy and Ann

DRUNKARD'S PATH: THE HISTORY OF A QUILT BLOCK

It's not often that a quilt block can be traced as far back as the days of Cleopatra. The Drunkard's Path, however, is one of the exceptions. Ancient Roman mosaics, unearthed in archaeological sites, reveal the twisty, turning design that is commonly referred to as the Drunkard's Path.

Though the design was around for centuries, quilters didn't use the Drunkard's Path block until the end of the nineteenth century, when it surfaced in England as a design called Robbing Peter to Pay Paul. When the Mayflower sailed from England to America, the block made the trip, too. Once in the new colonies, several different names were used to describe the block's new and different arrangements. Rocky Road to Kansas, Oregon Trail, Wanderer's Path, Boston Trail, and Wanderer in the Wilderness were just a few of the early aliases. Later on, Amish quilters added names such as Solomon's Puzzle, Old Maid's Dilemma, and Endless Trail to the growing list of block names. Today, all of these names are used, but the most popular is still Drunkard's Path.

Fortunately, the history of the Drunkard's Path (or whatever moniker you choose to give it) is well documented. The Drunkard's Path played an important part in two historical events—the Underground Railroad and the women's temperance movement.

The Drunkard's Path block played a significant role in the journey of slaves to freedom. The Underground Railroad could not openly broadcast information about where, when, and how runaway slaves could arrive safely at their destination. A system was therefore devised by which quilts were displayed, whether on a clothesline or over a porch railing, that contained hidden messages. The particular type of blocks in the quilt would tell the person making the journey what to do. When the Drunkard's Path block was displayed, the runaways would know to zigzag their path to make capture difficult.

In 1880 the Women's Christian Temperance Union (WCTU) was formed. These women were responsible for the closure of many saloons in their efforts to prohibit alcoholic beverages in the United States. The organization realized that a great way to raise money for awareness of their cause was to make quilts and raffle them off. While the Drunkard's Path block was not designed specifically for the temperance movement, the block does resemble the staggering walk of someone under the influence. Nothing is recorded about exactly when the Drunkard's Path name was created, but it might have come about to fit with, as strange as it sounds, the prohibition theme. Blue and white were the colors chosen by the WCTU. Most of the Drunkard's Path quilts from this period are seen with these two fabric colors.

Whatever its purpose, the Drunkard's Path remains a favorite of quilters today.

STARTER-BLOCK CONSTRUCTION BASICS

Our easy process for making the Drunkard's Path blocks begins with what we call a starter block. It consists of just two pieces: a square and a circle. The circle is appliquéd to the square and the resulting piece is then cut into quarters.

Each project in this book lists the number of starter blocks needed along with the sizes for the circles and background squares. Select at least two fabrics with high contrast so that the Drunkard's Path pattern will show up clearly.

After deciding on a project, follow the cutting instructions given. The cutting instructions will tell you to cut two different-sized squares for each starter block needed. The larger squares are for the background, and the smaller squares will be turned into circles (along with the interfacing).

To make each starter block:

1. Trace the circle pattern for the project you're making onto template plastic and cut it out exactly on the drawn line. The circle patterns for all the projects in this book are on pages 78–79. If you prefer, you can use a compass to make a perfect circle of the appropriate size. Do not trace around a bowl or saucer because most pottery isn't a perfect circle.

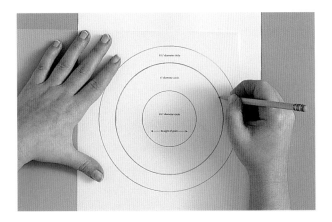

2. Using a fine-line pencil, or your preferred marking tool that will wash out, lay the circle template on the wrong side of the appropriate fabric square and trace around it.

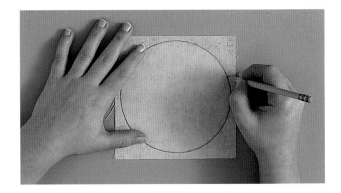

3. Lay the marked square wrong side up on top of the same-sized interfacing square; pin together on all four sides.

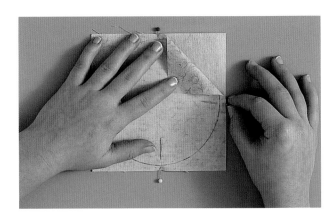

4. Stitch on the traced circle using 15 stitches per inch. Overlap the stitching at the beginning and end to secure the stitches. In order to stay on the marked line, it is helpful to use an open-toe presser foot and lift the foot frequently to adjust the pieces as you move around the curve.

5. When you have stitched completely around the circle, trim ⅛" from the stitching line. Cut a slit, approximately 2" to 3" long, in the center of the interfacing. Using appliqué scissors helps to ensure that only the interfacing will be cut and not the fabric beneath it.

6. Turn the circle right side out and gently push out the edges with a blunt instrument, such as a crochet hook.

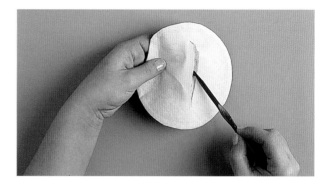

7. Carefully press the circle from the fabric side only, making sure the interfacing does not show from the front. Trim the interfacing from the back, leaving about ¼" around the edges.

8. Find the center of the larger background square by folding it in half. Use your fingernail to crease about a 2" length in the center of the fold.

STARTER-BLOCK CONSTRUCTION BASICS

9. Fold the square in half in the opposite direction and finger-press the center again. When the fabric is unfolded, there will be a small X marking the exact center of the square.

10. Follow the same procedure with the circle to produce an X in the center of it also. The X will be much more pronounced and easier to work with if you fold the circle on the grain of the fabric.

11. Match the centers of the circle and the square using the Xs as a guide. First, stick a pin through the right side of the circle directly through the center of the X. With right sides up, place the circle over the square, and insert the point of the pin through the X on the square.

12. Pin the circle to the right side of the background square with the centers exactly matched. Note: The grain line of the circle fabric should line up with the grain line of the background. This prevents bias edges when the squares are cut into quarters. The circle should be the same distance from all four edges of the square.

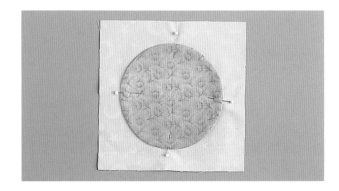

13. Stitch the circle in place using one of the following methods. Use invisible nylon thread on top or match the thread to the color of the circle fabric. The bobbin thread should match the color of the background square unless you are topstitching. If you topstitch, use a thread color that matches the circle in both the top and bobbin.

- Zigzag stitch
- Hand appliqué
- Blind hem stitch
- Decorative stitch, such as a buttonhole or another fancy stitch
- Topstitch very close to the edge

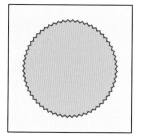

Zigzag stitch

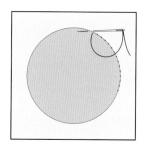

Hand appliqué

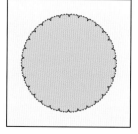

Blind hem stitch

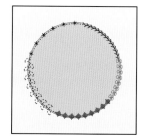

Decorative stitches

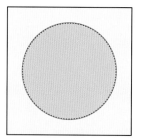

Topstitch

14. Once the circle is stitched in place, trim away the background fabric under the circle, trimming just inside the stitching line. Making the initial cut close to the seam allows the circle to remain intact so that it can be used for a smaller Drunkard's Path block or in another project.

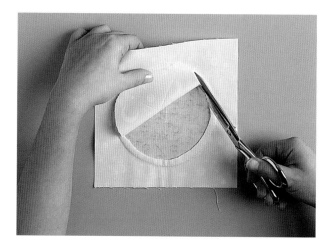

15. Measure and cut through the exact center of the block, both vertically and horizontally, to make four identical units. Because appliqué can cause a bit of distortion, it is a good idea to measure with two rulers butted up against each other to help ensure that both sides are equal.

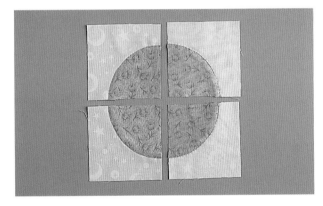

16. Already, with just these four units, the design possibilities of the Drunkard's Path are clearly visible. See "The Many Faces of the Drunkard's Path Block" beginning on the facing page for more variations.

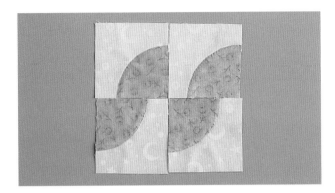

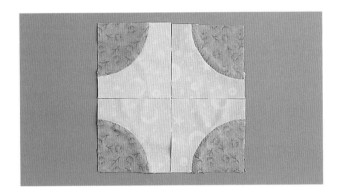

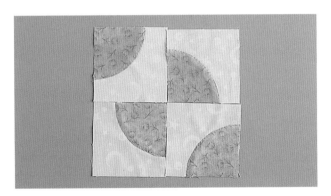

17. Once all the starter blocks are constructed and quartered into units, lay out the units according to the block diagram for the project you have chosen. Use a design wall, the floor, or a table. Stitch the units in each row together. Press the seams in each row in one direction and press the seams in opposite directions from row to row.

THE MANY FACES OF THE DRUNKARD'S PATH BLOCK

The possibilities for different designs with the Drunkard's Path are endless. Here are 80 different examples we have come up with, and there are probably many more! Where possible, a block name is given.

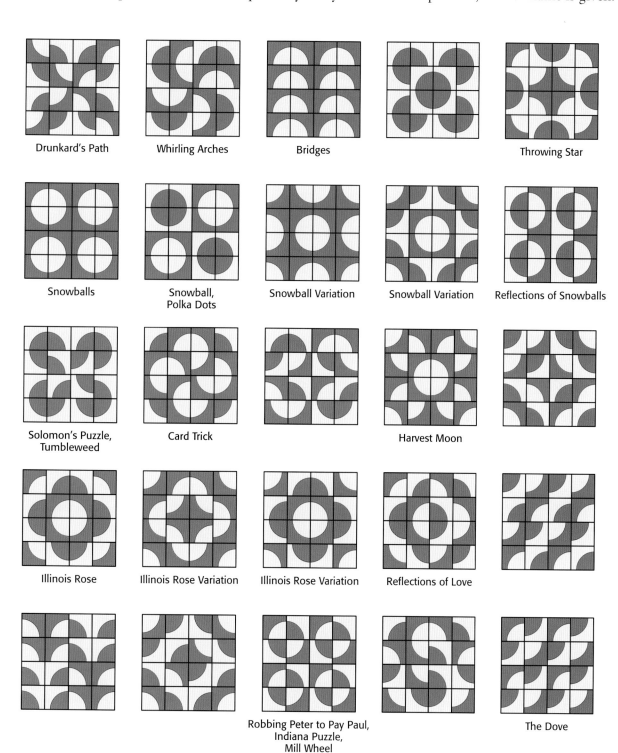

Drunkard's Path   Whirling Arches   Bridges   Throwing Star

Snowballs   Snowball, Polka Dots   Snowball Variation   Snowball Variation   Reflections of Snowballs

Solomon's Puzzle, Tumbleweed   Card Trick   Harvest Moon

Illinois Rose   Illinois Rose Variation   Illinois Rose Variation   Reflections of Love

Robbing Peter to Pay Paul, Indiana Puzzle, Mill Wheel   The Dove

11

Mushrooms

Reflections
of Mushrooms

Whirling Mushrooms

Links

Tumbling Circles

Fool's Puzzle

Ghost Walk,
Anna Dancing

Snowy Windows,
Dirty Windows

Harlequin

Wind Chimes

Snake Trail,
Falling Timbers Chain,
Vine of Friendship

Falling Timbers

Baby Bunting

King Tut's Crown,
Cleopatra's Puzzle

Anvils

Lollipop Trees

Once you've tried some of these variations, play around with the size of the circles for even more options. You can see in the pattern below how different the same block can look with this easy size alteration.

These patterns are exactly the same.
On the bottom block, smaller circles were used,
which drastically altered the look.

One way to see if you'll like a design once it's used in your quilt is to hold a folding mirror against the pattern and see what it will look like repeated.

ASSEMBLY AND FINISHING

Now that your quilt top is done, it is time to quilt it. Here are some basic instructions to get you on your way!

Marking the Quilting Design on the Quilt Top

If the quilt needs to be marked with a quilting pattern, mark it before the layers are basted together. Marking the pattern will not be necessary if the quilt will be stitched in the ditch, outline quilted, or free-motion quilted, such as with stipple quilting.

Test the marking tool on a piece of scrap fabric to make sure the marks can be removed easily. Masking tape can be used to mark straight-line quilting. Do not leave tape on the fabric overnight because it might leave a sticky residue.

Layering and Basting the Quilt

Before you can quilt your top, it must be layered with batting and backing and basted together.

1. To layer and baste the quilt, place the backing fabric right side down on a flat surface such as a table or a hard floor. Tape the fabric to the surface on all four sides. Masking tape works well.

2. Working around the quilt, lift up one section of tape at a time and gently pull and straighten out the fabric to get rid of any wrinkles. The fabric should be smooth and fairly taut.

3. Center the batting on top of the backing fabric and smooth it out with your hands.

4. Place the quilt top, right side up, over the batting. Make sure it is centered. Smooth out any wrinkles with your hands.

5. If you are machine quilting, pin baste with safety pins, starting in the center and working out. If you are hand quilting, thread baste, starting in the center and working out in all four directions.

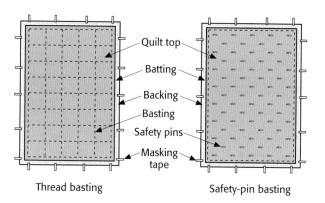

Thread basting   Safety-pin basting

Machine Quilting

For straight-line quilting, a walking foot will produce the best results. The walking foot helps feed all three quilt layers through the machine evenly, thus avoiding shifting and puckering. If free-motion quilting is used, a darning foot is needed and the feed dogs should be dropped. With free-motion quilting, the fabric can be guided in any direction necessary without turning the quilt.

Start quilting in the center of the quilt and work your way toward the outside edges. If the fabric print is very busy, don't waste time with intricate designs because they won't show up very well. Intricate designs show up best on plain fabric.

Hand Quilting

Hand quilting requires quilting needles, quilting thread, and a thimble. Most quilters support their quilts in a frame or hoop, although there are some hand quilters who quilt without any support.

1. Thread the quilting needle with an 18" length of quilting thread, knotting one end. Bring the needle down through the top layer only, about an inch from where you will start quilting. Bring the needle back up at the point where you will start. Give a gentle tug to pop the knot through the top layer and into the batting, locking the knot in place.

2. Take small, evenly spaced stitches through all three quilt layers. Rock the needle in an up-and-down motion, gathering three to four stitches on the needle. Make sure stitches are even on the front and back of the quilt. Put your non-quilting hand underneath the layers so you can feel the needle coming through the back of the quilt.

3. To finish, make a small knot close to your last stitch and then backstitch, taking the thread a needle's length through the batting. Gently tug the thread until the knot pops through the top layer and into the batting. Snip the thread at the surface of the quilt.

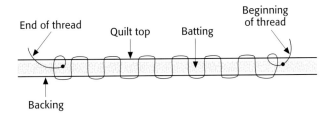

Cutting Bias Binding Strips

If a quilt has rounded corners or scalloped edges, you will need to cut your binding strips on the bias.

1. Lay your piece of binding fabric flat. Place the 45° line on your quilting ruler against the selvage edge of the fabric and make a cut.

2. Measuring from the initial cut, cut 2¼"-wide strips.

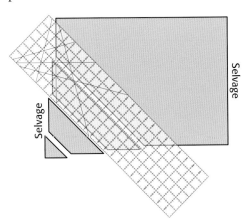

Binding the Quilt

1. Cut the binding strips as indicated in the quilt instructions.

2. Stitch the strips together as shown to make one long strip. A diagonal seam is preferred because it is less visible and less bulky. Trim ¼" from the stitching line and press the seams open.

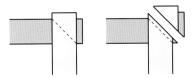

3. Trim one end of the strip at a 45° angle. Press the angled end under ¼". Press the strip in half lengthwise, wrong sides together.

4. Place the angled, folded-under end of the strip about one quarter of the way down on the right-hand side of the quilt. Stitch the binding to the quilt top using a ¼" seam allowance, leaving the first 8" of the binding unstitched. Stitch toward the corner of the quilt, stopping ¼" from the edge. Backstitch one or two stitches. Clip your thread.

5. Turn the quilt to stitch down the next side. Fold the binding strip up, away from the quilt, forming a 45°-angle fold at the corner and keeping the raw edges aligned.

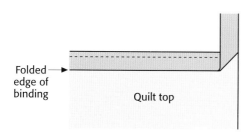

Folded edge of binding   Quilt top

6. Holding the fold in place, bring the strip back down onto itself, still keeping the raw edges aligned. Sew from the top of the fold, backstitching the first few stitches and continuing all the way down to ¼" from the next corner. Repeat the folding and stitching process at each corner.

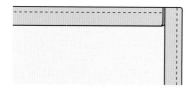

7. Stop stitching about 3" to 4" from the starting point of the binding. Measure the end of the binding so it overlaps the beginning by 1" to 2". Cut away the excess,

trimming at a 45° angle. Slip the end of the binding inside the beginning and finish sewing, backstitching at the end.

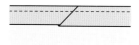

8. Trim the backing and batting even with the quilt top.

9. Fold the binding over the edge of the quilt to the back, just covering the edge of the machine stitching; blindstitch the binding in place. At each corner, a miter will form. Blindstitch these in place also.

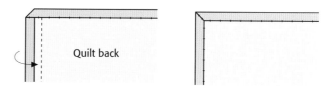

Quilt back

Labels

Last, but not least, a label should be added to the back of the quilt. Label composition should include name ("made by"), city and state, and the year the quilt was made. Other information that may be included: for whom the quilt was made; the occasion for which the quilt was made (wedding, anniversary, birth of baby, etc.); what pattern was used; the name of the quilt; how the quilt was made (quilted, pieced, or appliquéd by hand or machine); size of the quilt (comes in handy for entering shows or contests so you don't have to measure again); and washing instructions (especially nice when the quilt is given as a gift). If the quilt has a story behind it, include that as well.

We usually make our labels on plain muslin and then hand stitch them to the back of our quilts.

TEQUILA SUNRISE

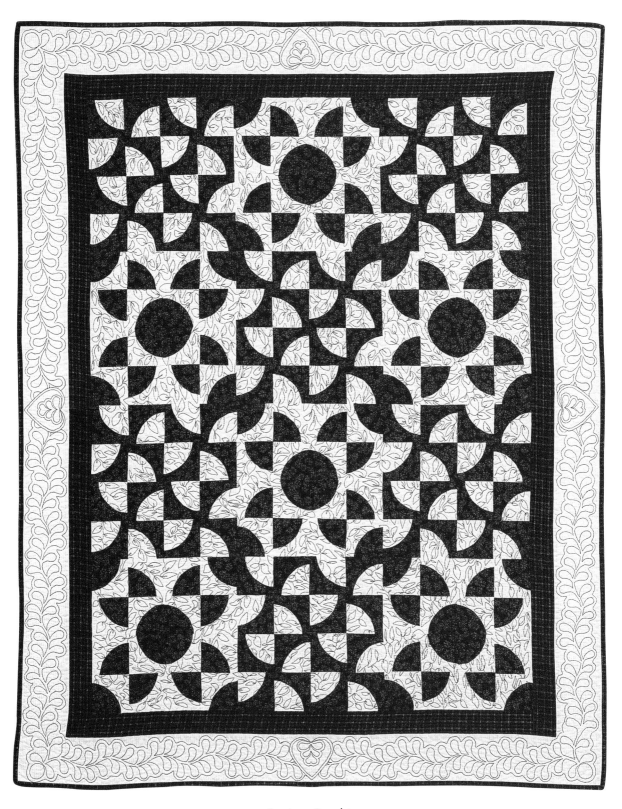

By Amy Sandrin
Finished quilt size: 51" x 64" • Finished block size: 13" x 13"

The Drunkard's Path block lends itself well to a two-colored quilt. Make sure the colors you select have good contrast, such as the red and white used here, so that the pattern will show up distinctly. I used two different blocks, Harvest Moon and Ghost Walk (which is also known as Anna Dancing). This was the first Drunkard's Path quilt I made using our machine-appliqué technique. It traveled with me as a sample quilt when Ann and I taught our Drunkard's Path class at the AQS show in Paducah, Kentucky. ~ Amy

Materials

Yardage is based on 42"-wide fabric unless otherwise noted.

- 2⅞ yards of red fabric for blocks, inner border, and binding
- 2⅞ yards of white fabric for blocks and outer border
- 3¼ yards of fabric for backing
- 57" x 70" piece of batting
- 3 yards of 22"-wide lightweight, nonfusible interfacing
- Template plastic
- Muslin or light-colored fabric, cut to desired size, for a quilt label

Cutting

All cutting dimensions include ¼" seam allowances.

From the red fabric, cut:

5 strips, 7½" x 42"; crosscut the strips into 24 squares, 7½" x 7½"

4 strips, 6" x 42"; crosscut the strips into 24 squares, 6" x 6"

5 strips, 2½" x 42"

6 strips, 2¼" x 42"

From the white fabric, cut:

5 strips, 7½" x 42"; crosscut the strips into 24 squares, 7½" x 7½"

4 strips, 6" x 42"; crosscut the strips into 24 squares, 6" x 6"

6 strips, 4½" x 42"

From the interfacing, cut:

14 strips, 6" x 22"; crosscut the strips into 48 squares, 6" x 6"

Making the Blocks

1. Trace the 5½"-diameter circle pattern on page 78 onto template plastic and cut it out.

2. Refer to "Starter-Block Construction Basics" on page 6 to construct the starter blocks. For the backgrounds, use the 7½" red and white squares. For the circles, use the template from step 1 and the 6" red, white, and interfacing squares. Make 24 starter blocks with white backgrounds and red circles. Make 24 starter blocks with red backgrounds and white circles. Cut the starter blocks into quarters. Each quarter should measure 3¾" x 3¾".

Make 24.

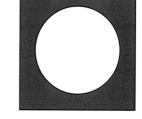
Make 24.

3. From the quartered units, construct the Harvest Moon and Ghost Walk blocks as shown. Make six of each. The blocks should measure 13½" x 13½".

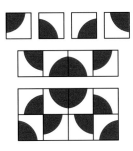

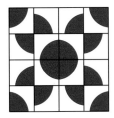

Harvest Moon block.
Make 6.

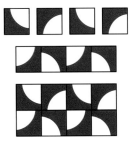

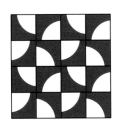

Ghost Walk block.
Make 6.

Assembling the Quilt

1. Lay out the blocks in four horizontal rows of three blocks each, alternating the Harvest Moon and Ghost Walk blocks in each row and from row to row as shown at right.

2. Sew the blocks in each row together. Press the seams of each row in one direction, alternating the direction from row to row. Sew the rows together. Press the seams in one direction.

Adding the Borders

1. Measure the width of the quilt top through the center. Trim two 2½" x 42" red strips to the length measured and sew them to the top and bottom of the quilt. Press the seam allowances toward the borders.

2. Measure the length of the quilt top through the center, including the just-added borders. Piece the remaining red border strips together end to end. From the pieced strip, cut two strips to the length measured and sew them to the sides of the quilt. Press the seam allowances toward the borders.

3. Follow steps 1 and 2 to add the 4½"-wide white border strips to the quilt top.

Finishing the Quilt

1. Piece the quilt backing so that it is approximately 6" longer and 6" wider than the quilt top.

2. Refer to "Layering and Basting the Quilt" on page 15 to layer the quilt top, batting, and backing; baste the layers together.

3. Hand or machine quilt as desired. This quilt was machine quilted with an overall leaf motif using free-motion quilting. This is a good design to use if you don't want to mark a pattern on the quilt top. A feather design was quilted in the borders.

4. When the quilting is complete, refer to "Binding the Quilt" on page 16 to bind the quilt using the 2¼" x 42" red strips.

5. Label the quilt and enjoy!

Quilt assembly

TOILE WAY

By Ann Frischkorn. Quilted by Char Hopeman.
Finished quilt size: 40½" x 40½" • Finished block size: 12" x 12"

I have a soft spot for floral designs. Combine that soft spot with my love of quilting and good things happen. I fell in love with the floral fabric in this quilt while perusing the vendor booths at the first annual Quilt Durango show and festival in Durango, Colorado. I tried cutting the fabric into the actual Drunkard's Path units, but I was disappointed when the flowers didn't show as much as I would have liked. One solution was to fussy cut the flowers and use them for a broderie-perse wreath. Broderie perse is an appliqué method in which whole or partial motifs are cut from fabric and appliquéd onto the background fabric. I found a yard of toile fabric languishing away in my stash that went beautifully with the floral pattern. I am totally thrilled with the elegance this quilt portrays. ~ Ann

Materials

Yardage is based on 42"-wide fabric unless otherwise noted.

- 2 yards of large-scale floral fabric for wreath blocks and outer border*
- 1⅝ yards of beige fabric for blocks
- ⅞ yard of toile fabric for blocks
- ¾ yard of maroon fabric for sashing, inner border, and binding
- 3 yards of fabric for backing
- 45" x 45" piece of batting
- 1 yard of 22"-wide lightweight, nonfusible interfacing
- 3½ yards of paper-backed fusible web*
- Template plastic
- Fine-line pencil or water-soluble marker
- Muslin or light-colored fabric, cut to desired size, for a quilt label

Amounts are approximate. The exact yardage required will depend on the size of the flower motifs.

Cutting

All cutting dimensions include ¼" seam allowances.

From the beige fabric, cut:

2 strips, 7" x 42"; crosscut the strips into 10 squares, 7" x 7"

2 strips, 5½" x 42"; crosscut the strips into 10 squares, 5½" x 5½"

2 strips, 13" x 42"; crosscut the strips into 4 squares, 13" x 13"

From the toile fabric, cut:

2 strips, 7" x 42"; crosscut the strips into 10 squares, 7" x 7"

2 strips, 5½" x 42"; crosscut the strips into 10 squares, 5½" x 5½"

From the interfacing, cut:

5 strips, 5½" x 22"; crosscut the strips into 20 squares, 5½" x 5½"

From the floral fabric, cut:

4 strips, 2¼" x 42" (The remainder will be used to cut the *broderie-perse* motifs.)

From the maroon fabric, cut:

8 strips, ¾" x 42"; crosscut 2 strips into 6 rectangles, ¾" x 12½"

5 strips, 2¼" x 42"

Making the Robbing Peter to Pay Paul Blocks

1. Trace the 5"-diameter circle pattern on page 79 onto template plastic and cut it out.

2. Refer to "Starter-Block Construction Basics" on page 6 to construct the starter blocks. For the backgrounds, use the 7" beige and toile squares. For the circles, use the template from step 1 and the 5½" beige, toile, and interfacing squares. Make 10 starter blocks with toile backgrounds and beige circles.

Make 10 starter blocks with beige backgrounds and toile circles.

Make 10. Make 10.

3. Cut the starter blocks into quarters. Each quarter should measure 3½" x 3½".

4. From the quartered units, construct the Robbing Peter to Pay Paul blocks as shown. Make five. The blocks should measure 12½" x 12½".

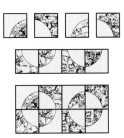

Robbing Peter to Pay Paul block.
Make 5.

Making the Broderie Perse Blocks

1. To help with the placement of the flower wreaths, draw an 8"-diameter circle in the center of each 13" beige square with a fine-line pencil or water-soluble marker. Tracing around an 8" saucer works great; you don't need a perfect circle in this instance, so using pottery will be fine here.

2. Follow the manufacturer's instructions to fuse the web to the wrong side of the remaining floral fabric.

3. Cut out flowers from the fused fabric, following the printed motifs and making sure to keep some leaves attached. If there are any edges that are really small or jagged, round them off with the scissors. This can be done while still maintaining the shape of the flower or leaf. The amount of flowers you need will depend on the size of the motifs.

4. Remove the paper from the back of the fabric. Arrange the flowers on the 13" squares using the marked circles as a guideline. It is beneficial if you can pin the squares up on a design wall and step back to view your progress. Cut out more flowers and leaves as needed to fill in any blank spaces. Fill in any small blank spots with leaves. Overlap the flowers and leaves for a natural appearance.

5. When the arrangement is complete, follow the manufacturer's instructions to fuse the motifs onto the beige squares. I actually ironed directly on my design wall so I didn't have to move anything.

6. Using threads that match each piece, stitch around all raw edges using a narrow, closely spaced satin stitch.

TIPS:
- I wanted to keep it interesting, so all four of my wreaths are arranged a little differently.
- It can be time consuming to change threads for each different flower or leaf color. Arrange the flowers on all four blocks and then stitch one color at a time. For example, stitch all the green shapes on all four blocks and then switch to another thread color.

7. After all the satin stitching is completed, trim the blocks to 12½" x 12½", keeping the wreaths centered.

Assembling the Quilt

1. Lay out the blocks in three horizontal rows of three blocks each, alternating the Robbing Peter to Pay Paul blocks and the *broderie perse* blocks. Sew the blocks in each row together, inserting a ¾" x 12½" maroon sashing strip between each block.

2. Measure the width of the block row. Trim two of the maroon ¾" x 42" strips to this length.

3. Sew the block rows together, inserting a sashing strip from step 2 between each row.

Adding the Borders

1. Measure the width of the quilt top through the center. Trim two ¾" x 42" maroon strips to the length measured and sew them to the top and bottom of the quilt. Press the seam allowances toward the blocks.

2. Measure the length of the quilt top through the center, including the just-added borders. Trim the remaining two ¾" x 42" maroon strips to the length measured and sew them to the sides of the quilt. Press the seam allowances toward the blocks.

3. Follow steps 1 and 2 to add the 2¼" x 42" floral border strips to the quilt top. Press the seam allowances toward the borders.

Quilt assembly

Note: If your top and bottom outer-border strips aren't at least 41" before trimming, or the width of the quilt top is more than the length of your strips, you will need to add an additional piece to the ends of the strips and then trim them to the required measurement.

Finishing the Quilt

1. Piece the quilt backing so that it is approximately 6" longer and 6" wider than the quilt top.

2. Refer to "Layering and Basting the Quilt" on page 15 to layer the quilt top, batting, and backing; baste the layers together.

3. Hand or machine quilt as desired. This quilt was long-arm machine quilted with a ½" cross-hatch in the wreath blocks. The Robbing Peter to Pay Paul blocks were stipple quilted in the beige fabric only. The toile fabric was left unquilted so it would stand out.

4. When the quilting is complete, refer to "Binding the Quilt" on page 16 to bind the quilt using the 2¼" x 42" maroon strips.

5. Label the quilt and enjoy!

TREK THROUGH THE JUNGLE

By Amy Sandrin. Quilted by Anne Spiotta.
Finished quilt size: 82½" x 82½" • Finished block size: 15" x 15"

I've always been drawn to animal prints. Something about the fabric brings out the cheetah woman in me. I tried arranging the blocks in this quilt about a billion different ways before deciding to stick with the original Drunkard's Path pattern. This project started out small and kept growing until it was bigger than the rain forest. Now it's not just a one-person nap quilt, but big enough to cover the lord of the jungle and a friend, too. ~ Amy

Materials

Yardage is based on 42"-wide fabric unless otherwise noted.

- 7⅜ yards of green, jungle-like fabric for blocks, sashing, and border
- 1¾ yards of snakeskin print fabric for border
- ⅞ yard *each* of five different animal print fabrics for blocks and sashing
- Enough tropical bird print fabric for three complete fussy-cut bird motifs
- 7½ yards of fabric for backing
- ¾ yard of fabric for binding
- 89" x 89" piece of batting
- 6 yards of 22"-wide lightweight, nonfusible interfacing
- Template plastic
- 2 small black buttons for snake eyes
- Muslin or light-colored fabric, cut to desired size, for a quilt label

> **TIP:**
> If you're having difficulty finding a variety of animal print fabrics locally, try the Internet. Type "animal print quilt fabric" into an Internet search engine and you'll find a large selection from which to choose.

Cutting

All cutting dimensions include ¼" seam allowances.

From the green fabric, cut:
18 strips, 8½" x 42"; crosscut the strips into 72 squares, 8½" x 8½"

4 strips, 7" x 42"; crosscut the strips into 18 squares, 7" x 7"

14 strips, 4¼" x 42"; crosscut the strips into 125 squares, 4¼" x 4¼"

From *each* of the five animal print fabrics, cut:
1 strip, 8½" x 42"; crosscut the strips into 4 squares, 8½" x 8½"

2 strips, 7" x 42"; crosscut the strips into 7 squares, 7" x 7"

From the snakeskin print fabric, cut:
8 strips, 7" x 42"; crosscut the strips into 37 squares, 7" x 7", for borders

1 rectangle, 4" x 5"

From the interfacing, cut:
30 strips, 7" x 22"; crosscut the strips into 90 squares, 7" x 7"

1 rectangle, 4" x 5"

From the binding fabric, cut:
9 strips, 2¼" x 42"

Making the Blocks

1. Trace the 6½"-diameter circle pattern on page 79 onto template plastic and cut it out.

2. Refer to "Starter-Block Construction Basics" on page 6 to construct the starter blocks. For the backgrounds, use the 8½" green and animal print squares. For the circles, use the template from step 1 and the 7" green, animal print, snakeskin print, and interfacing squares. Make 35 starter blocks with green backgrounds and animal print circles, 18 starter blocks with animal print backgrounds and green circles, and 37 starter blocks for the borders with green backgrounds and snakeskin print circles. Cut the starter blocks into quarters. Each quarter should measure 4¼" x 4¼".

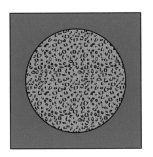

Make 35 total.

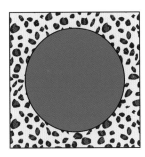

Make 18 total.

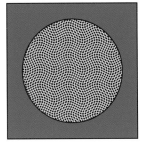

Make 37.

3. Using the quartered units with a green background and animal print circle and the quartered units with an animal print background and a green circle, construct the Drunkard's Path blocks as shown. Make two blocks *each* from four of the animal prints and one block from the remaining animal print (nine total). The blocks should measure 15½" x 15½". Set the remaining units aside for the sashing.

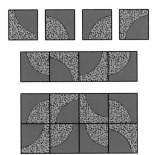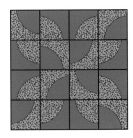

Drunkard's Path block.
Make 9 total.

Making the Sashing

1. To make the vertical sashing strips, stitch four of the remaining quartered units that were made with green backgrounds and animal print circles, and eight green 4¼" squares together as shown. Make six.

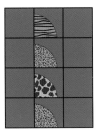

Vertical sashing strip.
Make 6.

2. To make the horizontal sashing strips, stitch 22 of the remaining quartered units that were made with green backgrounds and animal print circles, and 32 green 4¼" squares together as shown on the facing page. Make two.

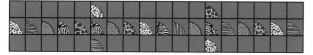

Horizontal sashing strip.
Make 2.

Assembling the Quilt

1. Lay out the blocks and sashing strips, placing the different animal print blocks as shown.

2. Sew the blocks and vertical sashing strips into rows as shown. Press the seams toward the sashing strips. Sew the rows and horizontal sashing strips together. Press the seams toward the horizontal sashing strips.

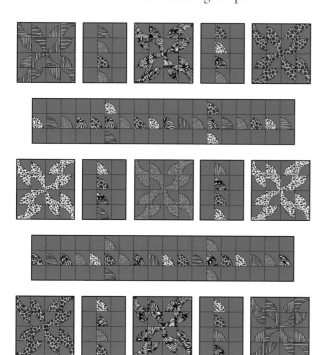

Adding the Borders

1. To make each border, lay out the quartered green background and snakeskin-print circle units as well as the remaining green 4¼" squares into rows as shown in step 3 below.

2. Sew the units in each row together. Press the seams in one row in one direction and the seams in the remaining row in the opposite direction.

3. Sew the two rows for each border together.

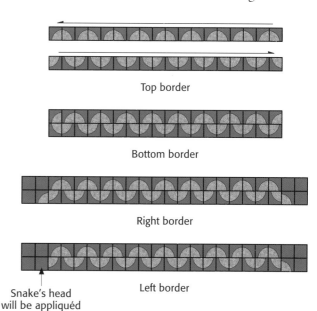

Top border

Bottom border

Right border

Left border

Snake's head
will be appliquéd
here.

4. Attach the borders to the quilt, bottom and top first, then each side, as shown.

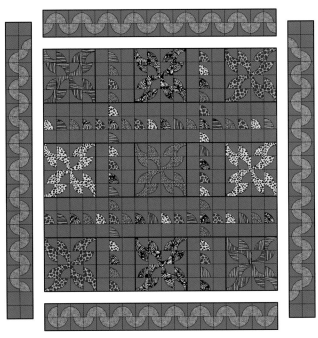

Quilt assembly

Making and Finishing the Snake's Head

1. Trace the snake head pattern on page 31 onto paper and cut it out.

2. Center the pattern on the wrong side of the 4" x 5" snake print rectangle; trace around the pattern.

3. Pin the 4" x 5" interfacing rectangle to the right side of the snake print rectangle. Using the same method you used for making the Drunkard's Path circles earlier, sew on the traced line, trim around the outside of the stitching line, and then make a small slit in the center of the interfacing and turn the head to the right side. Iron the piece flat.

4. Refer to the photo on page 26 to position and pin the head in place on the bottom-left corner of the quilt top. Appliqué the head in place.

5. Using red thread in your sewing machine and referring to the pattern and the photo as a guide, stitch lines for a forked tongue coming out of the snake's mouth. Sew two tiny black buttons to the head where indicated for the eyes.

Applying the Jungle Birds

1. Select three different bird motifs from the tropical bird fabric. Cut around them, leaving at least a ¼" seam allowance around the edges.

2. Using the same procedure you used to make the snake's head, make each bird into an appliqué unit by stitching on the outer edges of the motif.

3. Place the appliqués on the quilt as desired and appliqué them in place with invisible thread.

Finishing the Quilt

1. Piece the quilt backing so that it is approximately 6" longer and 6" wider than the quilt top.

2. Refer to "Layering and Basting the Quilt" on page 15 to layer the quilt top, batting, and backing; baste the layers together.

3. Hand or machine quilt as desired. This quilt was quilted with a jungle-like vine over the entire surface, excluding the snake. A wavy line was quilted close to the edges of the snake with curvy loops running through the middle of his body.

4. When the quilting is complete, refer to "Binding the Quilt" on page 16 to bind the quilt using the 2¼" x 42" binding-fabric strips.

5. Label the quilt, and get ready to discover the animal within you!

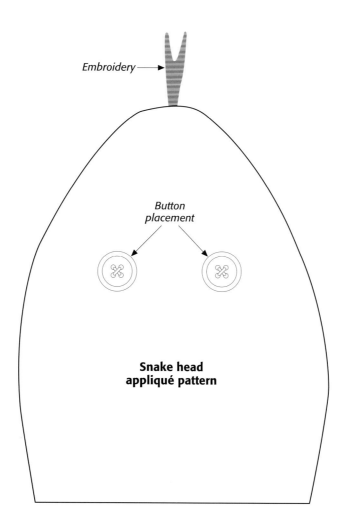

Embroidery →

Button placement

Snake head appliqué pattern

MERGING MIMOSAS

By Ann Frischkorn. Quilted by Mary Bojan.
Finished quilt size: 55" x 68" • Finished block size: 10" x 10"

I was inspired to make this quilt when I saw a photograph of an antique quilt by an unknown maker. The picture of the quilt was in a magazine article that featured the 100 masterpiece quilts from the Shelburne Museum. At first glance I could not tell what defined a block or how the quilt was pieced together, but after studying the picture for a while the light went on in my head. It appeared that one block was a Pineapple Log Cabin, but upon closer examination, I realized the block was actually a Drunkard's Path Snowball set on point. The sashing was made using flying-geese units and a connecting square set on point. The juncture where the sashing came together resembled a Pineapple block.

I made several design changes to the antique quilt to reflect my style and taste, including changing the color from the original cheddar cheese to a bright orange. I also eliminated the dogtooth border and made my border wider by adding sashing to the outside edges of the quilt. I hope you like it! ~ Ann

Materials

Yardage is based on 42"-wide fabric unless otherwise noted.

- 5¼ yards of orange fabric for blocks and sashing
- 3⅞ yards of white fabric for blocks, sashing, and binding
- 3½ yards of fabric for backing
- 61" x 74" piece of batting
- 1 yard of 22"-wide lightweight, nonfusible interfacing
- Template plastic
- Muslin or light-colored fabric, cut to desired size, for a quilt label

Cutting

All cutting dimensions include ¼" seam allowances.

From the orange fabric, cut:

3 strips, 5½" x 42"; crosscut the strips into 20 squares, 5½" x 5½"

7 strips, 6¼" x 42"; crosscut the strips into 40 squares, 6¼" x 6¼". Cut each square in half once diagonally to yield 80 triangles.

48 strips, 2¼" x 42"

From the white fabric, cut:

4 strips, 7½" x 42"; crosscut the strips into 20 squares, 7½" x 7½"

3 strips, 3" x 42"; crosscut the strips into 30 squares, 3" x 3"

23 strips, 2¾" x 42"

7 strips, 2¼" x 42"

From the interfacing, cut:

5 strips, 5½" x 22"; crosscut the strips into 20 squares, 5½" x 5½"

Making the Blocks

1. Trace the 5"-diameter circle pattern on page 79 onto template plastic and cut it out.

2. Follow steps 1–14 of "Starter-Block Construction Basics" on page 6 to construct the starter blocks. For the backgrounds, use the 7½" white squares. For the circles, use the template from step 1 and the 5½" orange and interfacing squares. *Do not cut the blocks into quarters.* Make 20 center units.

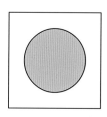

Make 20.

MERGING MIMOSAS

3. Sew an orange triangle to each side of each center unit, sewing opposite sides first. Press the seams toward the triangles. Trim each block to 10½" x 10½", keeping the circle centered.

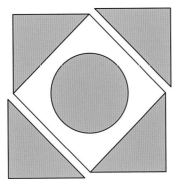

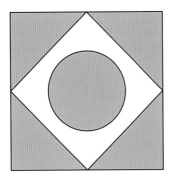

Snowball block.
Make 20.

4. To make the flying-geese units, cut all the 2¼" x 42" orange strips into triangles with a base of 3¾" as shown. Each strip should yield approximately 15 triangles.

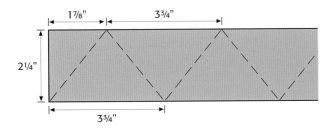

5. Using all the 2¾" x 42" white strips, cut triangles with a base of 4¼" as shown. Each strip should yield approximately 13 triangles.

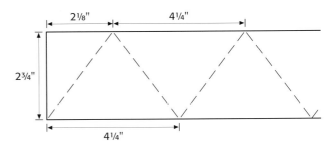

6. Refer to "Paper-Piecing Instructions" on page 35 to construct 98 flying-geese units using the pattern on page 37. Use the white triangles that were cut in step 5 for the pattern areas marked 1, 4, and 7, and the orange triangles that were cut in step 4 for the remaining areas.

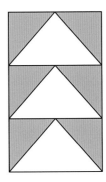

Flying-geese unit.
Make 98.

7. Paper piece 30 Square-on-Point blocks using the pattern on page 37. Use the 3" white squares for area 1 and the remaining orange triangles for areas 2–5.

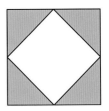

Square-on-Point block.
Make 30.

PAPER-PIECING INSTRUCTIONS

1. Using a lightweight paper that's easy to see through, such as tracing paper, make a copy of the pattern for each block you are going to sew. Martingale & Company sells foundation-piecing paper for this purpose, and you should be able to find it at any quilt shop. It can be used in any copy machine or laser printer.

2. Your fabric pieces should already be cut according to the quilt instructions, but it's not a bad idea to double-check and make sure the fabric pieces are large enough that they cover the entire area with seam allowances included. It's better to have a fabric piece that's too large rather than too small.

3. Place the wrong side of the fabric piece for area 1 against the unprinted side of area 1 on the paper pattern. Hold the pattern up to a light source to make sure all edges of the area are covered by the fabric and that there is at least ¼" extra on all edges. Pin the fabric in place.

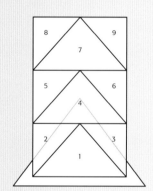

Place wrong side of fabric piece 1
against unmarked side
of paper pattern.

4. With right sides together, take the fabric for area 2 and place it over piece 1. Make sure the fabric extends beyond the stitching on all sides. Holding the fabric in place, flip the paper over to the printed side and stitch on the line between area 1 and area 2. Trim the excess fabric ¼" from the stitching.

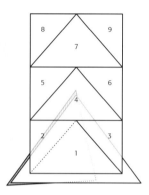

Place right side of fabric piece 2
against right side of piece 1.
Sew on the line between 1 and 2.

5. Open fabric piece 2, making sure it extends over the next seam allowance. Finger-press the piece open.

6. Working in numerical order, continue the process in the same manner until all pieces are sewn on.

7. Using a ruler and a rotary cutter, trim ¼" away from the sewing line on all four sides of the unit.

8. When the quilt is all put together, tear away the paper gently along the stitching lines.

Assembling the Quilt

1. Refer to the quilt assembly diagram to lay out the Snowball blocks, flying-geese units, and Square-on-Point blocks in 11 horizontal rows. Note that rows 1 and 2 alternate to make the quilt top.

2. Sew the blocks in each row together. Press all the seams in one row in the same direction, alternating direction from row to row. Sew the rows together. Press the seams in one direction.

Finishing the Quilt

1. Piece the quilt backing so that it is approximately 6" longer and 6" wider than the quilt top.

2. Refer to "Layering and Basting the Quilt" on page 15 to layer the quilt top, batting, and backing; baste the layers together.

3. Hand or machine quilt as desired. This quilt was long-arm machine quilted with freehand feathers and stipple quilting.

4. When the quilting is complete, refer to "Binding the Quilt" on page 16 to bind the quilt using the 2¼" x 42" white binding strips.

5. Label your quilt and enjoy!

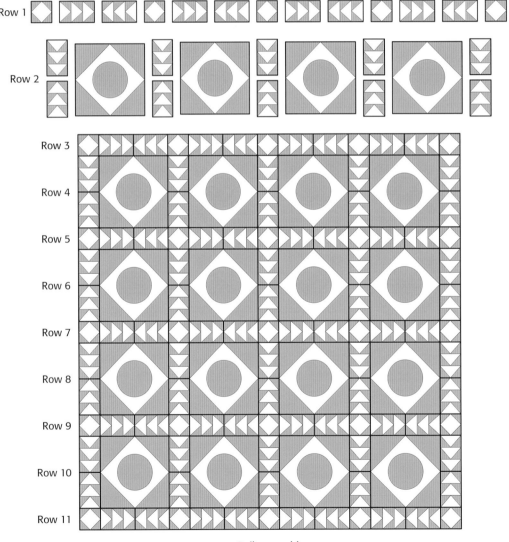

Quilt assembly

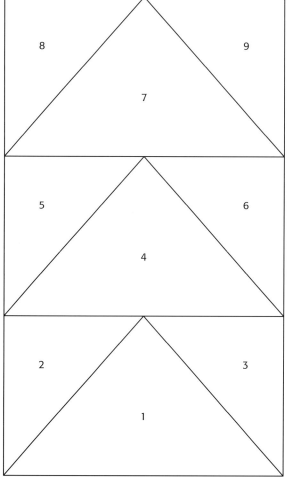

**Flying Geese
paper-piecing pattern**

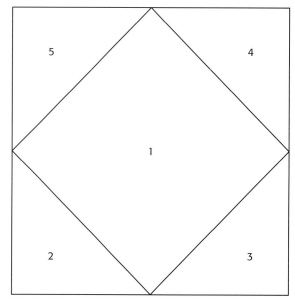

**Square-on-Point
paper-piecing pattern**

MIDORI SOUR

By Amy Sandrin. Quilted by Anne Spiotta.
Finished quilt size: 36¾" x 50¾" • Finished block size: 13¾" x 13¾"

I saw a picture of a stained-glass window in a magazine and thought it looked exactly like a Drunkard's Path quilt. Because I look at everything with the eyes of a quilter, I knew I had to make the stained-glass design into a quilt. Quilters are funny that way. For my color scheme, I chose bright greens and yellows, which reminded me of the drink called a Midori Sour. In order to achieve the stained-glass look, I appliquéd a circle onto a slightly larger black circle. The results are well worth the extra effort. ~ Amy

Materials

Yardage is based on 42"-wide fabric unless otherwise noted.

- 2 yards of black fabric for blocks, sashing, inner border, and binding
- 1¾ yards of green fabric for blocks and outer border
- 1¼ yards of yellow fabric for blocks
- 1⅞ yards of fabric for backing
- 43" x 57" piece of batting
- 3 yards of 22"-wide lightweight, nonfusible interfacing
- Template plastic
- Muslin or light-colored fabric, cut to desired size, for a quilt label

Cutting

All cutting dimensions include ¼" seam allowances.

From the green fabric, cut:

3 strips, 7½" x 42"; crosscut the strips into 12 squares, 7½" x 7½"

2 strips, 5½" x 42"; crosscut the strips into 12 squares, 5½" x 5½"

5 strips, 4" x 42"

From the yellow fabric, cut:

3 strips, 7½" x 42"; crosscut the strips into 12 squares, 7½" x 7½"

2 strips, 5½" x 42"; crosscut the strips into 12 squares, 5½" x 5½"

From the black fabric, cut:

4 strips, 6" x 42"; crosscut the strips into 24 squares, 6" x 6"

2 strips, 3¾" x 42"; crosscut the strips into 72 strips, ¾" x 3¾"

13 strips, ¾" x 42"; crosscut 11 strips into 22 strips, ¾" x 14¼"

4 strips, 1½" x 42"

5 strips, 2¼" x 42"

From the interfacing, cut:

8 strips, 6" x 22"; crosscut the strips into 24 squares, 6" x 6"

8 strips, 5½" x 22"; crosscut the strips into 24 squares, 5½" x 5½"

Making the Blocks

1. Trace the 5"- and 5½"-diameter circle patterns on pages 78 and 79 onto template plastic and cut them out.

2. Refer to "Starter-Block Construction Basics" on page 6 to construct the starter blocks. For the backgrounds, use the 7½" green and yellow squares. For the outer circles, use the 5½" circle template and the 6" black and interfacing squares. For the inner circles, use the 5" circle template and the 5½" green, yellow, and interfacing squares. Sew the black circles onto the background squares first, cut away the background fabric behind the circles, and then center and sew the inner circle to the outer circle; cut away the black fabric behind the inner circle. Make 12 starter

blocks with green backgrounds, black outer circles, and yellow inner circles. Make 12 starter blocks with yellow backgrounds, black outer circles, and green inner circles. Cut the starter blocks into quarters. Each quarter should measure 3¾" x 3¾".

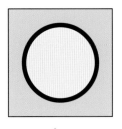 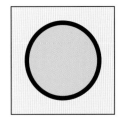

Make 12. Make 12.

3. From the quartered units and the ¾" x 3¾" and ¾" x 14¼" black strips, construct the Stained-Glass Drunkard's Path blocks. Make six. The blocks should measure 14¼" x 14¼".

Stained-Glass Drunkard's Path block.
Make 6.

4. Stitch a ¾" x 14¼" black strip to the bottom edge of four of the blocks.

Assembling the Quilt

1. Lay out the blocks in two vertical rows of three blocks each as shown, making sure that the two blocks on the bottom do *not* have the black sashing strip along the bottom edge.

2. Sew the blocks in each row together. Press the seams in one direction.

3. Measure the length of one row through the center. Piece the remaining two ¾" x 42" black strips together to make one long strip. Trim the strip to the length measured. Sew the rows together, inserting the strip between the rows.

Adding the Borders

1. Measure the width of the quilt top through the center. Trim two 1½" x 42" black strips to this measurement and sew them to the top and bottom of the quilt. Press the seam allowances toward the borders.

2. Measure the length of the quilt top through the center, including the just-added borders. Stitch the pieces that you cut off from the top and bottom borders to the remaining black 1½" x 42" strips. Trim the pieced strips to the length measured, trimming from the end farthest from the seam so the seam is not too close to the edge. Sew the strips to the sides of the quilt. Press the seam allowances toward the borders.

3. Follow steps 1 and 2 to add the 4"-wide green border strips to the quilt top.

Finishing the Quilt

1. Piece the quilt backing so that it is approximately 6" longer and 6" wider than the quilt top.

2. Refer to "Layering and Basting the Quilt" on page 15 to layer the quilt top, batting, and backing; baste the layers together.

3. Hand or machine quilt as desired. This quilt was machine quilted with a feather pattern on all the green portions, including the border. In the yellow portions, a simple wavy line was used close to the seam. The black areas were not quilted.

4. When the quilting is complete, refer to "Binding the Quilt" on page 16 to bind the quilt using the 2¼" x 42" black binding strips.

5. Label the quilt and enjoy!

Quilt assembly

ROAD LESS TRAVELED

By Ann Frischkorn. Quilted by Char Hopeman.

Finished quilt size: 32" x 32" • Finished Devil's Puzzle block size: 12" x 12" • Finished border block size: 4" x 4"

*S*crap quilts are the best. Not only did I get to reduce my leftovers when I made this quilt, I received the added benefit of tripping down memory lane. I used the remnants from the baby quilt I made when my niece was born; some fabric from a manly quilt I made for my husband's office; and even some fabric from when I was a rookie quilter more than 13 years ago. With all this reminiscing, I am surprised I found the time to finish this book!

When the blocks for this quilt were almost finished but not sewn together yet, I emailed a photo to my co-author, Amy. As I knew she would, she wrote back and said, "Something is missing." Two phone calls and lots of discussion later, voilà! Two heads are definitely better than one. A piping between the borders and the body of the quilt was the missing ingredient. This was exactly the kick this quilt needed. ~ Ann

Materials

Yardage is based on 42"-wide fabric unless otherwise noted.

- 1¼ yards *total* of assorted medium to dark fabrics for blocks (The more fabrics you choose, the scrappier the quilt will look.)
- ⅞ yard of medium beige fabric for border blocks
- ¾ yard of light beige fabric for blocks
- ½ yard of black fabric for piping and binding
- 1¼ yards of fabric for backing
- 38" x 38" piece of batting
- 1½ yards of 22"-wide lightweight, nonfusible interfacing
- Template plastic
- Muslin or light-colored fabric, cut to desired size, for a quilt label

Cutting

All cutting dimensions include ¼" seam allowances.

From the light beige fabric, cut:

3 strips, 5" x 42"; crosscut the strips into 20 squares, 5" x 5"

2 strips, 4" x 42"; crosscut the strips into 16 squares, 4" x 4"

From the medium beige fabric, cut:

3 strips, 5" x 42"; crosscut the strips into 18 squares, 5" x 5"

1 strip, 4" x 42"; crosscut the strip into 5 squares, 4" x 4"

2 strips, 2½" x 42"; crosscut the strips into 20 squares, 2½" x 2½"

From the assorted medium to dark fabrics, cut a *total* of:

21 squares, 5" x 5"

38 squares, 4" x 4"

From the black fabric, cut:

4 strips, ⅞" x 42"

4 strips, 2" x 42"

From the interfacing, cut:

12 strips, 4" x 22"; crosscut the strips into 59 squares, 4" x 4"

Making the Blocks

1. Trace the 3½"-diameter circle pattern on page 78 onto template plastic and cut it out.

2. Refer to "Starter-Block Construction Basics" on page 6 to construct the starter blocks. For the backgrounds, use the 5" light beige, medium beige, and assorted medium to dark squares. For the circles, use the template from step 1 and the 4" light beige, medium

beige, assorted medium to dark, and interfacing squares. Make 20 starter blocks with light beige backgrounds and assorted medium/dark circles. Make 18 starter blocks with medium beige backgrounds and assorted medium/dark circles. Make 16 starter blocks with assorted medium/dark backgrounds and light beige circles. Make 5 starter blocks with assorted medium/dark backgrounds and medium beige circles. Cut the starter blocks into quarters. Each quarter should measure 2½" x 2½".

Make 20 total.   Make 18 total.   Make 16 total.   Make 5 total.

3. From the quartered units and the 2½" medium beige squares, make four Devil's Puzzle blocks, 20 Border Unit A blocks, and eight Border Unit B blocks as shown. The Devil's Puzzle blocks should measure 12½" x 12½". The border blocks should measure 4½" x 4½".

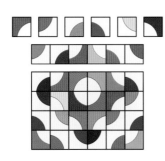

Devil's Puzzle block.
Make 4.

Border Unit A   Border Unit B
block.   block.
Make 20.   Make 8.

Assembling the Quilt

1. Lay out the Devil's Puzzle blocks in two horizontal rows of two blocks each as shown.

2. Sew the blocks in each row together. Press the seams in the first row in one direction, alternating the direction in the next row. Sew the rows together.

Adding the Piping

1. Measure the width of the quilt top through the center. Cut *each* of the four ⅞" x 42" black strips to the length measured.

2. Press each strip in half lengthwise, wrong sides together.

3. Using a ⅛" seam allowance, baste a strip to the top and bottom edges of the quilt top, aligning the raw edges. Do not press. Repeat to baste the remaining two strips to the sides of the quilt top. Again, do not press.

Adding the Borders

1. Stitch border blocks A and B together as shown to make the border strips. Make two top and bottom border strips and two side border strips.

Top and bottom borders.
Make 2.

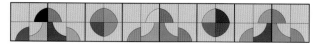

Side borders.
Make 2.

2. Pin the top and bottom borders over the piping on the top and bottom edges of the quilt top. Pin carefully to make sure the seams in the border blocks line up with the seams in the Devil's Puzzle blocks; stitch.

Press the seam allowances toward the borders. Repeat to stitch the side borders to the sides of the quilt top. Press the seam allowances toward the borders.

Finishing the Quilt

1. Cut the backing fabric so that it is approximately 6" longer and 6" wider than the quilt top.

2. Refer to "Layering and Basting the Quilt" on page 15 to layer the quilt top, batting, and backing; baste the layers together.

3. Hand or machine quilt as desired. This quilt was long-arm machine quilted with stippling in the beige areas. The dark areas were left free of quilting to make them stand out.

4. When the quilting is complete, refer to "Binding the Quilt" on page 16 to bind the quilt using the 2" x 42" black binding strips.

5. Label the quilt and enjoy!

Quilt assembly

KAHLÚA AND CREAM

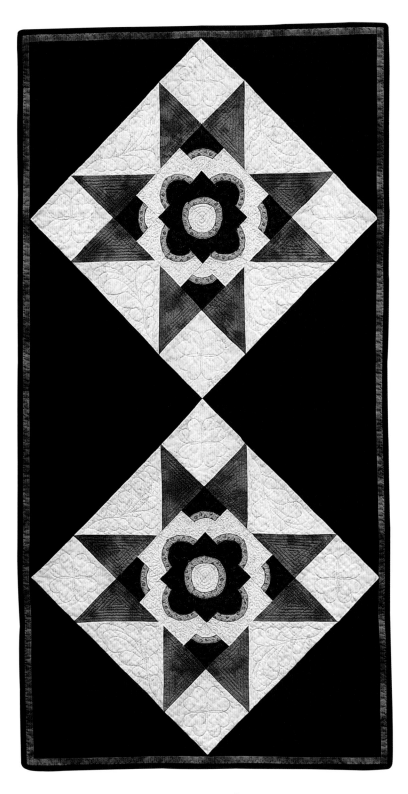

By Amy Sandrin
Finished quilt size: 26½" x 52" • Finished block size: 17½" x 17½"

*T*his quilt was made for my good friend Terri Clark. No, she's not the country singer, but she is a fiction writer and one of the best movie reviewers I know. I wanted to incorporate a Drunkard's Path block, called Illinois Rose, as the centerpiece of a larger block. The finished block became a variation of the Ohio Star block. As Murphy's Law would have it, by the time I finished this quilt, which was for Terri's bathroom, her color scheme had changed. Luckily those colors migrated to her kitchen, so it will find a spot somewhere in her home after all. ~ Amy

Materials

Yardage is based on 42"-wide fabric unless otherwise noted.

- 1⅛ yards of black fabric for blocks, corner and side setting triangles, and binding
- ¾ yard of white fabric for blocks
- ⅝ yard of brown fabric for blocks and border
- ¼ yard of beige fabric for blocks
- 1⅞ yards of fabric for backing
- 32" x 57" piece of batting
- ½ yard of 22"-wide lightweight, nonfusible interfacing
- Template plastic
- Muslin or light-colored fabric, cut to desired size, for a quilt label

Cutting

All cutting dimensions include ¼" seam allowances.

From the black fabric, cut:

1 strip, 5½" x 42"; crosscut the strip into 4 squares, 5½" x 5½". Trim the remainder of the strip to 3" wide and cut 4 squares, 3" x 3".

1 square, 26¾" x 26¾"; cut the square in half twice diagonally to yield 4 side setting triangles. You will use 2 and have 2 left over.

1 strip, 13⅝" x 42"; crosscut the strip into 2 squares, 13⅝" x 13⅝". Cut each square in half once diagonally to yield 4 corner triangles.

5 strips, 2¼" x 42"

From the white fabric, cut:

1 strip, 5½" x 42"; crosscut the strip into 4 squares, 5½" x 5½". Trim the remainder of the strip to 3" wide and cut 4 squares, 3" x 3".

3 strips, 4¾" x 42"; crosscut the strips into:

8 squares, 4¾" x 4¾"

8 rectangles, 4¾" x 9½"

From the beige fabric, cut:

1 strip, 4" x 42"; crosscut the strip into 8 squares, 4" x 4"

From the brown fabric, cut:

12 strips, 4¾" x 42"; crosscut the strips into 16 squares, 4¾" x 4¾"

5 strips, 1" x 42"

From the interfacing, cut:

2 strips, 3" x 22"; crosscut the strips into 8 squares, 3" x 3"

2 strips, 4" x 22"; crosscut the strips into 8 squares, 4" x 4"

Making the Blocks

1. Trace the 2½"- and 3½"-diameter circle patterns on pages 78 and 79 onto template plastic and cut them out.

2. Refer to "Starter-Block Construction Basics" on page 6 to construct the starter blocks. For the backgrounds, use the 5½" black and white squares. For the outer circles, use the 3½" template from step 1 and the 4" beige and interfacing squares. For the inner circles, use

the 2½" template from step 1 and the 3" black, white, and interfacing squares. Sew the beige circles onto the background squares first, cut away the background fabric behind the circles, and then center and sew the inner circle to the outer circle; cut away the beige fabric behind the inner circle. Make four starter blocks with black backgrounds, beige outer circles, and white inner circles. Make four starter blocks with white backgrounds, beige outer circles, and black inner circles. Cut the starter blocks into quarters. Each quarter should measure 2¾" x 2¾".

Make 4.

Make 4.

3. From the quartered units, make two block center units as shown. The center units should measure 9½" x 9½".

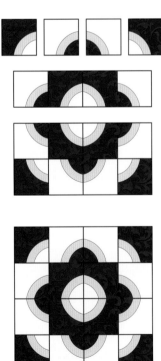

Make 2.

4. Draw a line from corner to corner on the wrong side of each 4¾" brown square. With right sides together, place a square on one end of each 4¾" x 9½" white rectangle; sew on the marked line. Trim ¼" from the stitching line. Press the brown triangle toward the corner. Repeat on the opposite end of each rectangle.

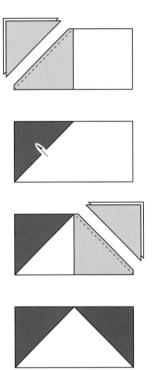

5. Stitch a unit from step 4 to opposite sides of the center units as shown. Stitch a 4¾" white square to each end of the remaining four units as shown, and stitch them to the top and bottom of each center unit to complete the Illinois Rose Star blocks.

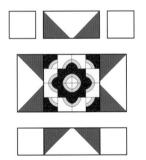
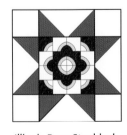

Illinois Rose Star block.
Make 2.

Assembling the Quilt

1. Sew a side setting triangle and a corner triangle to opposite sides of each block as shown. Add a corner triangle to one remaining side of each block. Stitch the two halves together.

2. Trim the edges ¼" from the block points.

Adding the Borders

1. Measure the width of the quilt top through the center. Trim two 1" x 42" brown strips to the length measured and sew them to the top and bottom of the quilt top. Press the seam allowances toward the borders.

2. Measure the length of the quilt top through the center, including the just-added borders. Piece the remaining brown border strips together end to end. From the pieced strip, cut two strips to the length measured and sew them to the sides of the quilt. Press the seam allowances toward the borders.

Finishing the Quilt

1. Piece the quilt backing so that it is approximately 6" longer and 6" wider than the quilt top.

2. Refer to "Layering and Basting the Quilt" on page 15 to layer the quilt top, batting, and backing; baste the layers together.

3. Hand or machine quilt as desired. For this quilt I used feather motifs and echo quilting throughout.

4. When the quilting is complete, refer to "Binding the Quilt" on page 16 to bind the quilt using the 2¼" x 42" black binding strips.

5. Label the quilt and enjoy!

UNDER THE OVERPASS

By Ann Frischkorn
Finished quilt size: 13½" x 13½" • Finished block size: 2" x 2"

I was noodling around with some Drunkard's Path blocks on my design wall when I accidentally stumbled upon this pattern. It is similar to the Card Trick block. I love the optical illusion the pattern creates, kind of like a complicated cloverleaf intersection on the highway.

I have always had a fascination with miniature quilts and have wanted to make at least a dozen to fill the only blank wall in my sewing room. One down, 11 to go. Keep on trucking! ~ Ann

Materials

Yardage is based on 42"-wide fabric unless otherwise noted.

- ½ yard of dark red fabric for blocks, inner border, and binding
- ⅜ yard of pale yellow fabric for blocks and outer border
- ⅝ yard of fabric for backing
- 19½" x 19½" piece of batting
- ⅜ yard of 22"-wide lightweight, nonfusible interfacing
- Template plastic
- Muslin or light-colored fabric, cut to desired size, for a quilt label

Cutting

All cutting dimensions include ¼" seam allowances.

From the dark red fabric, cut:

2 strips, 2½" x 42"; crosscut the strips into 25 squares, 2½" x 2½"

2 strips, 1¾" x 42"

2 strips, 2¼" x 42"

From the pale yellow fabric, cut:

2 strips, 3" x 42"; crosscut the strips into 25 squares, 3" x 3"

2 strips, 1" x 42"

From the interfacing, cut:

4 strips, 2½" x 22"; crosscut the strips into 25 squares, 2½" x 2½"

Making the Blocks

1. Trace the 2"-diameter circle pattern on page 78 onto template plastic and cut it out.

2. Refer to "Starter-Block Construction Basics" on page 6 to construct the starter blocks. For the backgrounds, use the 3" pale yellow squares. For the circles, use the template from step 1 and the 2½" dark red and interfacing squares. Make 25 starter blocks with pale yellow backgrounds and dark red circles. Cut the starter blocks into quarters. Each quarter should measure 1½" x 1½".

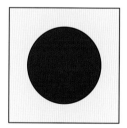

Make 25.

UNDER THE OVERPASS

3. From the quartered units, construct 16 Card Trick variation blocks, five Snowball blocks, and four Mountain Pass blocks as shown. The blocks should measure 2½" x 2½".

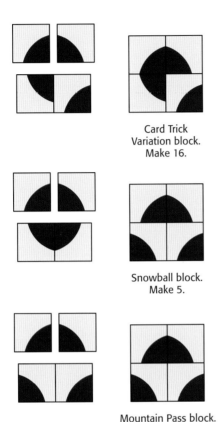

Card Trick
Variation block.
Make 16.

Snowball block.
Make 5.

Mountain Pass block.
Make 4.

Assembling the Quilt

1. Lay out the blocks in five horizontal rows of five blocks each as shown.

2. Sew the blocks in each row together. Press all the seams in one row in the same direction, alternating the pressing direction from row to row. Sew the rows together. Press the seams in one direction.

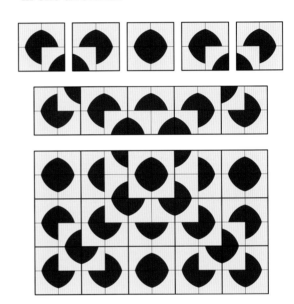

Adding the Borders

1. Measure the width of the quilt top through the center. From one 1¾" x 42" dark red strip, cut two strips to the length measured and sew them to the top and bottom of the quilt. Press the seam allowances toward the borders.

2. Measure the length of the quilt top through the center, including the just-added borders. From the remaining 1¾" x 42" dark red strip, cut two strips to the length measured and sew them to the sides of the quilt. Press the seam allowances toward the borders.

3. Follow steps 1 and 2 to add the 1"-wide pale yellow strips to the quilt top.

Finishing the Quilt

1. Cut the fabric for the backing so it is 6" longer and 6" wider than the quilt top.

2. Refer to "Layering and Basting the Quilt" on page 15 to layer the quilt top, batting, and backing; baste the layers together.

3. Hand or machine quilt as desired. For this quilt, I machine quilted a stipple design in the pale yellow portion only. I left the red circles unquilted because I wanted them to stand out. I quilted graduating circles on the borders and stipple quilted around them.

4. When the quilting is complete, refer to "Binding the Quilt" on page 16 to bind the quilt using the 2¼" x 42" dark red binding strips.

5. Label your quilt and enjoy!

Quilt assembly

SCENIC OVERLOOK

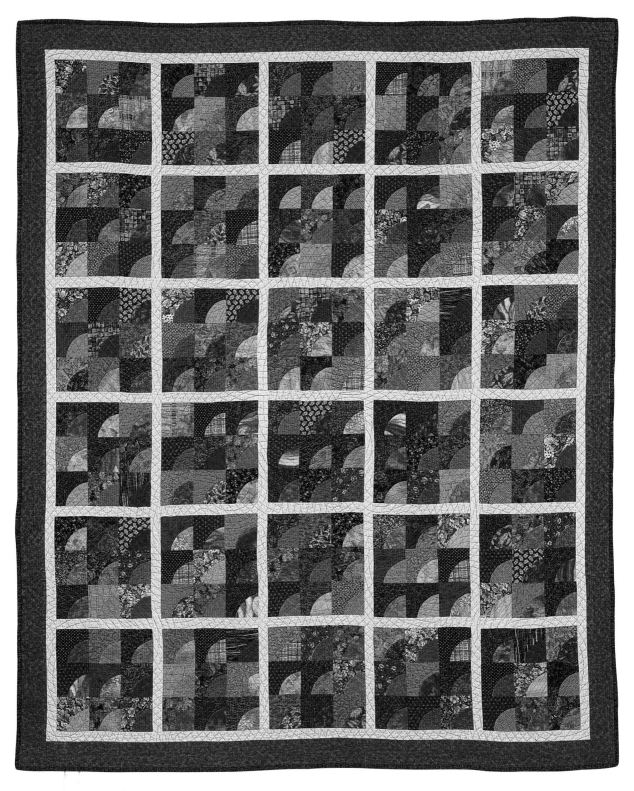

By Amy Sandrin
Finished quilt size: 59¾" x 70½" • Finished block size: 9¾" x 9¾"

One of my favorite colors in the world is brown, closely followed by orange. I decided to combine these colors in a "nap" quilt just for me to use when I watch reality shows on TV. The Drunkard's Path pattern I chose is called Dirty Windows. I thought it would be a great idea to set off a block with such a name by adding sashing around each one so it resembled a "dirty" Attic Window block. Pick two of your favorite colors to make this quilt, and snuggle up to watch your favorite shows. ~ Amy

Materials

Yardage is based on 42"-wide fabric unless otherwise noted.

- 3¼ yards *total* of assorted brown fabrics for blocks
- 1¾ yards *total* of assorted orange fabrics for blocks
- 1 yard of beige fabric for sashing and inner border
- ¾ yard of orange fabric for outer border
- 3⅝ yards of fabric for backing
- ⅝ yard of brown fabric for binding
- 66" x 76" piece of batting
- 3 yards of 22"-wide lightweight, nonfusible interfacing
- Template plastic
- Muslin or light-colored fabric, cut to desired size, for a quilt label

Cutting

All cutting dimensions include ¼" seam allowances.

From the assorted brown fabrics, cut a *total* of:
68 squares, 7½" x 7½"

From the assorted orange fabrics, cut a *total* of:
68 squares, 5½" x 5½"

From the beige fabric, cut:
18 strips, 1½" x 42"; crosscut 8 strips into 24 rectangles, 1½" x 10¼"

From the interfacing, cut:
17 strips, 5½" x 22"; crosscut the strips into 68 squares, 5½" x 5½"

From the orange border fabric, cut:
7 strips, 3" x 42"

From the brown binding fabric, cut:
7 strips, 2¼" x 42"

Making the Blocks

1. Trace the 5"-diameter circle pattern on page 79 onto template plastic and cut it out.

2. Refer to "Starter-Block Construction Basics" on page 6 to construct the starter blocks. For the backgrounds, use the 7½" brown squares. For the circles, use the 5½" orange and interfacing squares. Make a total of 68 starter blocks. Cut the starter blocks into quarters. Each quarter should measure 3¾" x 3¾".

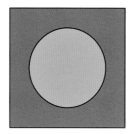

Make 68 total.

3. From the quartered units, construct 30 Dirty Windows blocks. The blocks should measure 10¼" x 10¼".

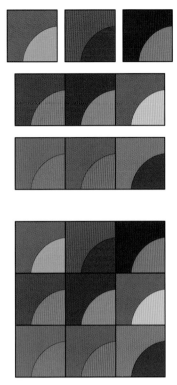

Dirty Windows block.
Make 30.

Assembling the Quilt

1. Lay out the blocks in six horizontal rows of five blocks each as shown. Make sure all the blocks are going in the correct direction, with the quarter circle in the bottom right of each square. Sew the blocks together, inserting a 1½" x 10¼" beige rectangle between each block. Press the seams toward the beige rectangles.

2. Measure the length of one block row through the center. Piece the 1½" x 42" beige strips together end to end. From the pieced strip, cut seven strips to the length measured for the horizontal sashing and the top and bottom border strips.

3. Sew the block rows and the beige strips together, alternating the sashing and block rows as shown. Press the seams toward the beige strips.

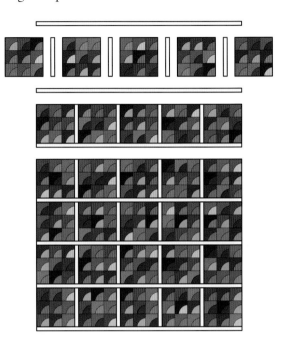

Adding the Borders

1. Measure the length of the quilt top through the center. From the remainder of the 1½"-wide beige pieced strip, cut two strips to the length measured and sew them to the sides of the quilt. Press the seam allowances toward the borders.

2. Measure the length of the quilt top through the center. Piece the orange 3" x 42" strips together end to end. From the pieced strip, cut two strips to the length measured, and sew them to the top and bottom of the quilt. Press the seam allowances toward the borders.

3. Measure the length of the quilt top through the center, including the just-added borders. From the remainder of the pieced orange strip, cut two strips to the length measured, and sew them to the sides of the quilt. Press the seam allowances toward the borders.

Finishing the Quilt

1. Piece the quilt backing so that it is approximately 6" longer and 6" wider than the quilt top.

2. Refer to "Layering and Basting the Quilt" on page 15 to layer the quilt top, batting, and backing; baste the layers together.

3. Hand or machine quilt as desired. For this quilt, I machine quilted an allover wavy grid pattern, spacing the lines ½" apart.

4. When the quilting is complete, refer to "Binding the Quilt" on page 16 to bind the quilt using the 2¼" x 42" brown binding strips.

5. Label the quilt and get ready to watch your favorite television shows.

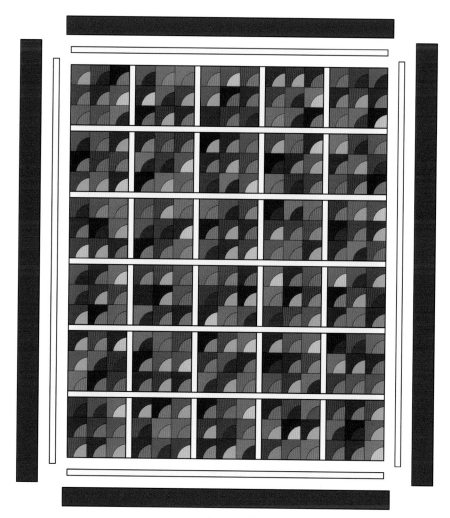

Quilt assembly

PARK PLACE

By Ann Frischkorn
Finished quilt size: 42½" x 49" • Finished Drunkard's Path block size: 13" x 13"
Finished Half Drunkard's Path block size: 6½" x 13"

*Y*ou always remember your firsts. This blue-and-white quilt is the first Drunkard's Path quilt I
made using our machine-appliqué technique. I used this quilt as a sample when I taught a
Drunkard's Path class at the Cotton Cottage Quilt Shop in Wheaton, Illinois. I wanted a
smaller, lap-sized quilt so I could cozy up with it while I played Monopoly with my kids on those long winter
afternoons. Park Place may be one of the most sought-after properties on the game board, but when we're playing Monopoly, "Park Place"—the quilt—is the most sought-after property in our house. Those who claim it first
believe it will bring them luck. ~ Ann

Materials

*Yardage is based on 42"-wide fabric unless otherwise
noted.*

- 2¼ yards of blue fabric for blocks, outer border, and binding
- 1⅝ yards of off-white fabric for blocks and inner border
- 3 yards of fabric for backing
- 48½" x 55" piece of batting
- 2 yards of 22"-wide lightweight, nonfusible interfacing
- Template plastic
- Muslin or light-colored fabric, cut to desired size, for a quilt label

Cutting

All cutting dimensions include ¼" seam allowances.

From the blue fabric, cut:

3 strips, 7½" x 42"; crosscut the strips into 15 squares, 7½" x 7½"

3 strips, 6" x 42"; crosscut the strips into 15 squares, 6" x 6"

5 strips, 3½" x 42"

5 strips, 2¼" x 42"

From the off-white fabric, cut:

3 strips, 7½" x 42"; crosscut the strips into 15 squares, 7½" x 7½"

3 strips, 6" x 42"; crosscut the strips into 15 squares, 6" x 6"

4 strips, 2½" x 42"

From the interfacing, cut:

10 strips, 6" x 22"; crosscut the strips into 30 squares, 6" x 6"

Making the Blocks

1. Trace the 5½"-diameter circle pattern on page 78 onto template plastic and cut it out.

2. Refer to "Starter-Block Construction Basics" on page 6 to construct the starter blocks. For the backgrounds, use the 7½" blue and off-white squares. For the circles, use the template from step 1 and the 6" blue, off-white, and interfacing squares. Make 15 starter blocks with blue backgrounds and off-white circles. Make 15 starter blocks with off-white backgrounds and blue circles. Cut the starter blocks into quarters. Each quarter should measure 3¾" x 3¾".

Make 15.

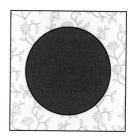
Make 15.

3. From the quartered units, construct six Drunkard's Path blocks and three Half Drunkard's Path blocks as shown. The full blocks should measure 13½" x 13½". The half blocks should measure 7" x 13½".

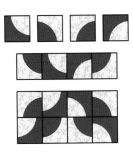

Drunkard's Path block.
Make 6.

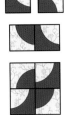

Half Drunkard's Path block.
Make 3.

Assembling the Quilt

1. Lay out the blocks in three horizontal rows of two Drunkard's Path blocks and one Half Drunkard's Path block as shown.

2. Sew the blocks in each row together. Press all the seams in one row in the same direction, alternating the pressing direction from row to row. Sew the rows together. Press the seams in one direction.

Adding the Borders

1. Measure the width of the quilt top through the center. Trim two 2½" x 42" off-white border strips to the length measured and sew them to the top and bottom of the quilt. Save the pieces that were trimmed off because they will be used to piece the side borders. Press the seam allowances toward the borders.

2. Measure the length of the quilt top through the center, including the just-added borders. Stitch the pieces that you cut off from the top

and bottom borders to the remaining off-white 2½" x 42" strips. Trim the pieced strips to the length measured, trimming from the end farthest from the seam so the seam is not too close to the edge. Sew the strips to the sides of the quilt. Press the seam allowances toward the borders.

3. Measure the width of the quilt top through the center. Cut two 3½" x 42" blue strips to the length measured and stitch them to the top and bottom of the quilt. Press the seam allowances toward the borders.

4. Measure the length of the quilt top through the center, including the just-added borders. Piece the remaining 3½" x 42" blue strips together end to end. From the pieced strip, cut two strips to the length measured and sew them to the sides of the quilt. Press the seam allowances toward the borders.

Finishing the Quilt

1. Piece the quilt backing so that it is approximately 6" longer and 6" wider than the quilt top.

2. Refer to "Layering and Basting the Quilt" on page 15 to layer the quilt top, batting, and backing; baste the layers together.

3. Hand or machine quilt as desired. For this quilt I machine quilted a scroll design in the white fabric. In the blue fabric I quilted ¼" inside the seam. A feather design was quilted in the borders.

4. When the quilting is complete, refer to "Binding the Quilt" on page 16 to bind the quilt using the 2¼" x 42" blue binding strips.

5. Label the quilt and challenge someone to a rousing game of Monopoly!

Quilt assembly

TAILGATE PARTY

By Amy Sandrin. Quilted by Char Hopeman.
Finished quilt size: 43" x 43" • Finished block size: 12" x 12"

I designed the layout for these string-pieced Drunkard's Path blocks on graph paper first, fully intending the colors to be in the purple, blue, and green families. When I saw the finished drawing, the design looked exactly like a watermelon. There was no doubt in my mind that the colors had to be changed to pink and green. Not only does this pattern incorporate two different techniques, but it also uses two different sizes of the same Drunkard's Path block.

Using the string-pieced method is a great way to use up a lot of scrap fabrics, but it does take a little extra time. If time is of the essence, and you still want to make this pattern, find a green striped fabric and use it instead of piecing all the greens together. ~ Amy

Materials

Yardage is based on 42"-wide fabric unless otherwise noted.

- 2⅛ yards *total* of assorted green fabrics for blocks and borders
- 2 yards of pink fabric for blocks
- 1½ yards of fabric for backing
- ½ yard of green fabric for binding
- 49" x 49" piece of batting
- 1⅞ yards of 22"-wide lightweight, nonfusible interfacing
- Template plastic
- Muslin or light-colored fabric, cut to desired size, for a quilt label

Cutting

All cutting dimensions include ¼" seam allowances.

From the pink fabric, cut:

4 strips, 7" x 42"; crosscut the strips into 20 squares, 7" x 7"

7 strips, 4" x 42"; crosscut the strips into 64 squares, 4" x 4"

From the assorted green fabrics, cut:

Approximately 100 strips, each at least 20" long and varying in width from ¾" to 1¼"

From the interfacing, cut:

5 strips, 5½" x 22"; crosscut the strips into 20 squares, 5½" x 5½"

10 strips, 3" x 22"; crosscut the strips into 64 squares, 3" x 3"

From the green binding fabric, cut:

5 strips, 2¼" x 42"

Making the String-Pieced Squares

1. Stitch the assorted green strips together side by side until you have a piece that measures a width of at least 5½".

2. Crosscut the pieced strip into 5½"-wide segments. Square up each segment to 5½" x 5½".

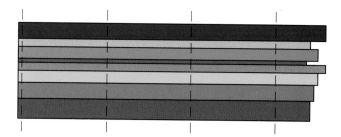

3. Repeat steps 1 and 2 until you have 20 squares, 5½" x 5½". These squares will be used to make the larger circles in the Drunkard's Path starter blocks.

4. Follow steps 1 and 2 above, but make each strip at least 3" wide. Crosscut the pieced strip into segments 3" wide and square up each segment to 3" x 3". You will need 64 pieced squares. These squares will be used when making the smaller circles in the Drunkard's Path starter blocks.

TIP:
If you have a bunch of scraps that are less than 20" long, you can still use them; it will just take a little longer to assemble all the pieces. If you are going to use small scraps, they must be at least 6" long or 3½" long so you can trim them up.

Making the Blocks

1. Trace the 2½"- and 5"-diameter circle patterns on page 79 onto template plastic and cut them out.

2. Refer to "Starter-Block Construction Basics" on page 6 to construct the starter blocks. For the backgrounds, use the 7" and 4" pink squares. For the circles, use the templates from step 1, the 5½" and 3" string-pieced squares, and the 5½" and 3" interfacing squares. Make 20 large starter squares and 64 small starter squares, each with pink backgrounds and green string-pieced circles. Cut the starter blocks into quarters. The quartered units from the large squares should measure 3½" x 3½". The quartered units from the small squares should measure 2" x 2".

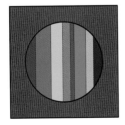

Make 20.   Make 64.

3. From the large quartered units, construct five Solomon's Puzzle Variation I blocks as shown. From the small quartered units, construct four Solomon's Puzzle Variation II blocks as shown. The blocks should measure 12½" x 12½".

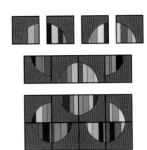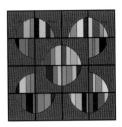

Solomon's Puzzle
Variation I block.
Make 5.

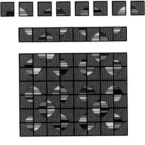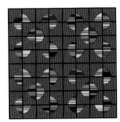

Solomon's Puzzle
Variation II block
Make 4.

Assembling the Quilt

1. Lay out the blocks in three horizontal rows of three blocks each, alternating the variation I and variation II blocks in each row.

2. Sew the blocks in each row together. Press all the seams in one row in the same direction, alternating the direction from row to row.

Sew the rows together. Press the seams in one direction.

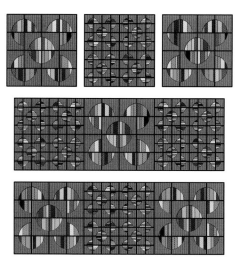

Adding the Borders

1. Measure the length of the quilt top through the center. Cut all the remaining green strip scraps so they measure exactly 4" long. Sew these strips together side by side until you have two strips that are 4" wide and the length measured. Sew them to the sides of the quilt. Press the seam allowances toward the borders.

2. Measure the width of the quilt top through the center, including the just-added borders. Sew together more green 4" scrap strips until you have two strips that are 4" wide and the width measured. Sew them to the top and bottom of the quilt. Press the seam allowances toward the borders.

Finishing the Quilt

1. Piece the quilt backing so that it is approximately 6" longer and 6" wider than the quilt top.

2. Refer to "Layering and Basting the Quilt" on page 15 to layer the quilt top, batting, and backing; baste the layers together.

3. Hand or machine quilt as desired. For this quilt, an overall vine motif was used in keeping with the watermelon theme.

4. When the quilting is complete, refer to "Binding the Quilt" on page 16 to bind the quilt using the 2¼" x 42" green binding strips.

5. Label the quilt, and get ready for a picnic or a tailgate party featuring watermelon as the dessert.

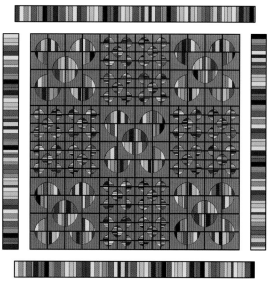

Quilt assembly

TRIP AROUND THE WORLD

By Ann Frischkorn
Finished quilt size: 49½" x 49½" • Finished block size: 3" x 3"

*S*ometimes you just need to be selfish. This is one of the rare times I made a quilt for myself. Typically, I give the quilts I make away as gifts, but I wanted one that I could display in my family room. My living room is maroon and my family room is green. I designed this quilt with both rooms in mind. Luckily, when it was finished, this quilt fits beautifully in either room. I have always wanted to try my hand at a scalloped border and the rows in this quilt just called for scallops. ~ Ann

Materials

Yardage is based on 42"-wide fabric unless otherwise noted.

- 3 yards of beige fabric for blocks and binding
- 2 yards of maroon fabric for blocks, corner and side setting triangles, and borders
- 1¼ yards of green fabric for blocks
- 3⅛ yards of fabric for backing
- 56" x 56" piece of batting
- 2⅞ yards of 22"-wide lightweight, nonfusible interfacing
- Template plastic
- Freezer paper
- Muslin or light-colored fabric, cut to desired size, for a quilt label

Cutting

All cutting dimensions include ¼" seam allowances.

From the beige fabric, cut:

4 strips, 7" x 42"; crosscut the strips into 20 squares, 7" x 7"

5 strips, 6" x 42"; crosscut the strips into 25 squares, 6" x 6"

1 square, 36" x 36"

From the green fabric, cut:

2 strips, 7" x 42"; crosscut the strips into 11 squares, 7" x 7"

3 strips, 6" x 42"; crosscut the strips into 14 squares, 6" x 6"

From the maroon fabric, cut:

3 strips, 7" x 42"; crosscut the strips into 14 squares, 7" x 7"

1 strip, 6" x 42"; crosscut the strip into 6 squares, 6" x 6"

5 strips, 4" x 42"

2 strips, 5½" x 42"; crosscut the strips into 8 squares, 5½" x 5½". Cut each square in half twice diagonally to yield 32 side setting triangles.

1 strip, 5¼" x 42"; crosscut the strip into 2 squares, 5¼" x 5¼". Cut each square in half once diagonally to yield 4 corner triangles.

From the interfacing, cut:

15 strips, 6" x 22"; crosscut the strips into 45 squares, 6" x 6"

Making the Blocks

1. Trace the 5½"-diameter circle pattern on page 78 onto template plastic and cut it out.

2. Refer to "Starter-Block Construction Basics" on page 6 to construct the starter blocks. For the backgrounds, use the 7" beige, green, and maroon squares. For the circles, use the template from step 1 and the 6" beige, green, maroon, and interfacing squares. Make 14 blocks with beige backgrounds and green circles. Make 14 blocks with maroon backgrounds and beige circles. Make 11 blocks with green backgrounds and beige circles. Make six blocks with beige backgrounds and

TRIP AROUND THE WORLD

maroon circles. Cut the starter blocks into quarters. Each quarter should measure 3½" x 3½".

Make 14. Make 14.

Make 11. Make 6.

Assembling the Quilt

1. Lay out the quartered units and the side setting triangles into 18 diagonal rows as shown.

2. Sew the units and triangles in each row together. Press all the seams in one row in the same direction, alternating the pressing direction from row to row.

3. Sew a corner triangle to each corner of the quilt top. If necessary, trim the edges of the quilt top ¼" from the points of the quartered units.

Adding the Borders

1. Measure the width of the quilt top through the center. Piece two of the 4" x 42" maroon border strips together end to end. From the pieced strip, cut two strips to the length measured and sew them to the top and bottom of the quilt. Press the seam allowances toward the borders.

2. Measure the length of the quilt top through the center, including the just-added borders. Piece the remaining maroon border strips together end to end. From the pieced strip, cut two strips to the length measured and sew them to the sides of the quilt. Press the seam allowances toward the borders.

Quilt assembly

3. Trace the scalloped border pattern on page 69 onto freezer paper and cut it out. The template will be used to mark the curves for the scallop onto the border. There will be five scallops per side. The end scallops merge to form a nice rounded corner.

4. Iron the freezer-paper template in place on the right side of the border. Line up the bottom edge of the template along the seam line between the border and the block units. Mark the scallops with a light-colored pencil that won't easily rub off. This pencil mark will be covered by the binding, so it's OK if it isn't easily removed. You will cut along the lines *after* the quilting is complete.

Finishing the Quilt

1. Piece the quilt backing so that it is approximately 6" longer and 6" wider than the quilt top.

2. Refer to "Layering and Basting the Quilt" on page 15 to layer the quilt top, batting, and backing; baste the layers together.

3. Hand or machine quilt as desired. For this quilt, I machine quilted feathers along every row. When quilting in the borders, keep your quilting pattern about ½" away from the marked scallop lines.

4. When the quilting is complete, refer to "Cutting Bias Binding Strips" on page 16 to cut the 36" beige square into 2¼"-wide bias strips. Refer to "Binding the Quilt" on page 16 to attach the binding. A little extra care is needed when sewing on a scalloped binding. Align the raw edges of the binding with the drawn line on the border. As the binding is stitched on, ease it around the outer curves, taking care not to stretch it. At the inside point of the curve, lift the presser foot and pivot, taking care that there are no pleats or puckers. Clip the seam allowance at the inner

point up to the stitching line. When the binding is attached, trim away the excess border, backing, and batting, leaving ¼" to fill the binding.

5. Label the quilt and keep this one for yourself!

Scalloped border pattern

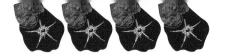

Martini & Rosey

By Ann Frischkorn and Amy Sandrin. Quilted by Ann Frischkorn.
Finished quilt size: 25½" x 34½" • Finished block size: 9" x 9"

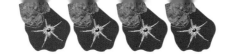

*E*ver since we were beginning quilters, we have always wanted to work on a project together. One perfectionist is bad enough, but add two identical twins with the same genetic compulsions to the mix, and well, it's not pretty. One night we stayed up until 1:30 to get the background on this quilt just right. When we got up the next morning, we hated it and were sure the evil quilt fairies had visited us. With only hours before Amy's plane left, we started from scratch and arrived at the design shown here. To tell the truth, we probably reworked this background two or three times, but who's counting? When we finally got it right, unbelievably, we argued over who was going to keep it. That debate is still in progress. ~ Amy & Ann

Materials

Yardage is based on 42"-wide fabric unless otherwise noted.

- ½ yard *total* of assorted blue fabrics ranging from light to dark for squares (We used about 20 different blues.)
- ½ yard of light brown fabric for border and binding
- ⅜ yard of dark brown fabric for Drunkard's Path blocks and squares
- ¼ yard of medium dark green fabric for Drunkard's Path blocks
- ¼ yard of medium green fabric for Drunkard's Path blocks and border
- ¼ yard *total* of assorted green fabrics ranging from light to dark for squares (We used about 12 different greens.)
- ¼ yard of very light blue fabric for Drunkard's Path blocks
- ¼ yard of light blue fabric for Drunkard's Path blocks
- ¼ yard of medium blue fabric for border
- ¼ yard of medium brown fabric for Drunkard's Path blocks and border
- ¼ yard *total* of assorted brown fabrics ranging from light to dark for squares (We used about 8 different browns.)
- ⅛ yard *total* of assorted shades of fabrics in *each* of the following colors for appliqués: purple, orange, pink, red, yellow, and green

- 1 yard of fabric for backing
- 32" x 42" piece of batting
- ⅜ yard of 22"-wide lightweight, nonfusible interfacing
- 1 yard of paper-backed fusible web
- Template plastic
- Brown or black fine-tipped permanent marker
- Muslin or light-colored fabric, cut to desired size, for a quilt label

Cutting

All cutting dimensions include ¼" seam allowances.

From the very light blue fabric, cut:
1 strip, 5½" x 42"; crosscut the strip into 4 squares, 5½" x 5½"

From the light blue fabric, cut:
1 strip, 4" x 42"; crosscut the strip into 4 squares, 4" x 4"

From the assorted blue fabrics, cut a *total* of:
64 squares, 2¾" x 2¾"

From the medium blue fabric for border, cut:
2 strips, 1½" x 42"; crosscut the strips into:
　　2 strips, 1½" x 20"
　　1 strip, 1½" x 24"

From the medium dark green fabric, cut:
2 squares, 5½" x 5½"
2 squares, 4" x 4"

From the medium green fabric, cut:
2 squares, 5½" x 5½"
2 squares, 4" x 4"
2 strips, 1½" x 9½"

From the assorted green fabrics, cut a *total* of:
24 squares, 2¾" x 2¾"

From the dark brown fabric, cut:
1 square, 4" x 4"
1 strip, 1½" x 42"; crosscut the strip into:
   2 strips, 1½" x 6½"
   1 strip, 1½" x 24"

From the medium brown fabric, cut:
1 square, 5½" x 5½"

From the assorted brown fabrics, cut a *total* of:
16 squares, 2¾" x 2¾"

From the light brown fabric, cut:
4 strips, 1" x 42"; crosscut the strips into:
   2 strips, 1" x 23"
   2 strips, 1" x 33"
4 strips, 2¼" x 42"

From the interfacing, cut:
2 strips, 4" x 22"; crosscut the strips into 9 squares, 4" x 4"

Making the Blocks

1. Trace the 3½"-diameter circle pattern on page 78 onto template plastic and cut it out.

2. Refer to "Starter-Block Construction Basics" on page 6 to construct the starter blocks. For the backgrounds, use the 5½" very light blue, medium dark green, medium green, and medium brown squares. For the circles, use the template from step 1 and the 4" light blue, medium green, medium dark green, dark brown, and interfacing squares. Make four blocks with very light blue backgrounds and light blue circles. Make two blocks with medium dark green backgrounds and medium green circles. Make two blocks with medium green

backgrounds and medium dark green circles. Make one block with a medium brown background and a dark brown circle. Cut the starter blocks into quarters. Each quarter should measure 2¾" x 2¾".

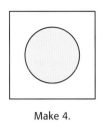
Make 4.

Make 2.

Make 2.

Make 1.

3. From the quartered units, construct one *each* of the Dove block and the Whirling Arches block as shown. The blocks should measure 9½" x 9½". Set the quarter units from the brown circle aside.

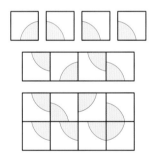

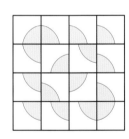
Dove block.
Make 1.

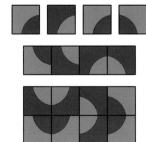

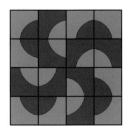
Whirling Arches block.
Make 1.

Assembling the Quilt

1. Refer to the illustrations to assemble the assorted blue, green, and brown squares, the Dove block, the Whirling Arches block, and the brown quartered units into the blue, green, and brown sections as shown. For the blue and green sections, arrange the squares into smaller sections as shown. Sew the squares in each smaller section into rows. Press all the seams in one row in the same direction, alternating the pressing direction from row to row. Then, sew the sections and the block together. Press the seams in one direction. For the brown section, sew the brown squares and the quartered units into two rows. Press all the seams in one row in the same direction, alternating the pressing direction in each row. Sew the rows together.

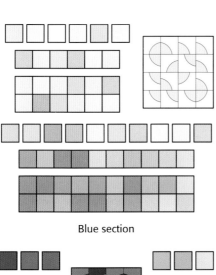

Blue section

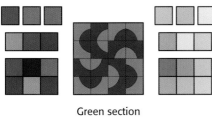

Green section

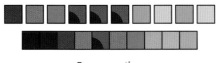

Brown section

2. Sew the three sections together as shown to complete the quilt top.

Adding the Borders

1. Sew the 1" x 23" light brown strips to the top and bottom of the quilt. Press the seam allowances toward the borders. Sew the 1" x 33" light brown strips to the sides of the quilt. Press the seam allowances toward the borders.

2. Sew the 1½" x 24" medium blue strip to the top of the quilt. Press the seam allowance toward the border. Sew the 1½" x 24" dark brown strip to the bottom of the quilt. Press the seam allowance toward the border.

3. Refer to the quilt assembly diagram on page 74 to piece a 1½" x 20" medium blue strip, a 1½" x 9½" medium green strip, and a 1½" x 6½" dark brown strip together to make a side border. Make two. Stitch the strips to the

sides of the quilt top, making sure the corresponding color sections line up. Press the seam allowances toward the borders.

Quilt assembly

Appliquéing the Flowers

1. Follow the manufacturer's instructions to adhere the paper-backed fusible web to the wrong side of the various appliqué fabrics.

2. Trace the flower and leaf patterns on pages 76 and 77 onto plain paper and cut them out. The dashed lines inside the patterns are the quilting lines. Also cut approximately twelve 2", 3", and 4" squares from the pink fabrics to be used for the spiral roses.

3. Lay the paper patterns onto the wrong sides of the appropriate fabrics and trace around the shapes with a pen or pencil. You should be tracing right onto the fusible-web paper. Cut out the shapes and remove the paper backing.

4. For the stems of the daylilies, cut a strip of green fabric ¼" x 42" wide. The strip will be cut into various lengths after the flowers have been arranged satisfactorily.

5. To make the spiral roses, cut off the four corners of each square at various widths. Don't try to be perfect.

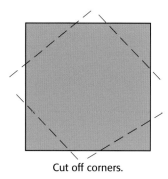

Cut off corners.

6. Starting on any edge, make a spiral cut with your scissors, turning the block while cutting in a circular motion. Practice on paper first to gain confidence.

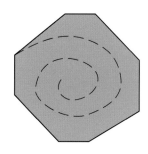

7. When the first cut is complete, go back and cut along the same line again, making the cut a bit wider. This will help the spiral show up. When the cut is complete there will be two spirals: a very skinny spiral that can be saved and used in another project, and the spiral rose that will be used for this project.

8. Arrange the flowers and leaves on the quilt top, referring to the photo on page 70 as necessary. Cut the ¼"-wide green strip to the lengths needed for the daylily stems. Pin each piece in place. Remember to overlap flowers for a more realistic effect. If you have a design wall, pin the pieces in place right to the wall. This will take a lot of pins, but pieces shouldn't be ironed in place until they are all arranged satisfactorily. Step back from the design often to view the arrangement from afar.

9. When the arrangement is pleasing, iron the pieces in place. If you can, iron directly on the design wall so no pieces accidentally shift.

10. Using a brown or black permanent marker, make tiny dots in the center of the daisies.

Finishing the Quilt

1. Refer to "Layering and Basting the Quilt" on page 15 to layer the quilt top, batting, and backing; baste the layers together.

2. Hand or machine quilt the background sections. For this quilt, the sky was quilted with swirls. The grass was quilted using a free-form leaf design, and the dirt was stipple quilted.

3. Even though the pieces are fused to the top, stitch all the appliqué pieces very close to the edges to hold them down securely.

4. Machine quilt the detail in all the flowers and the vines in the leaves using the lines inside the templates as a reference. We used a contrasting thread to give more visual impact. The roses were quilted with lines that followed the direction of the spirals.

5. Stitch curlicue vines among the morning glories.

6. Quilt stems for the tall purple flowers behind the daisies.

Daylilies

Morning glories

7. When the quilting is complete, refer to "Binding the Quilt" on page 16 to bind the quilt using the 2¼" x 42" light brown binding strips.

8. Label the quilt and enjoy your garden year-round!

Daisies

Appliqué Patterns

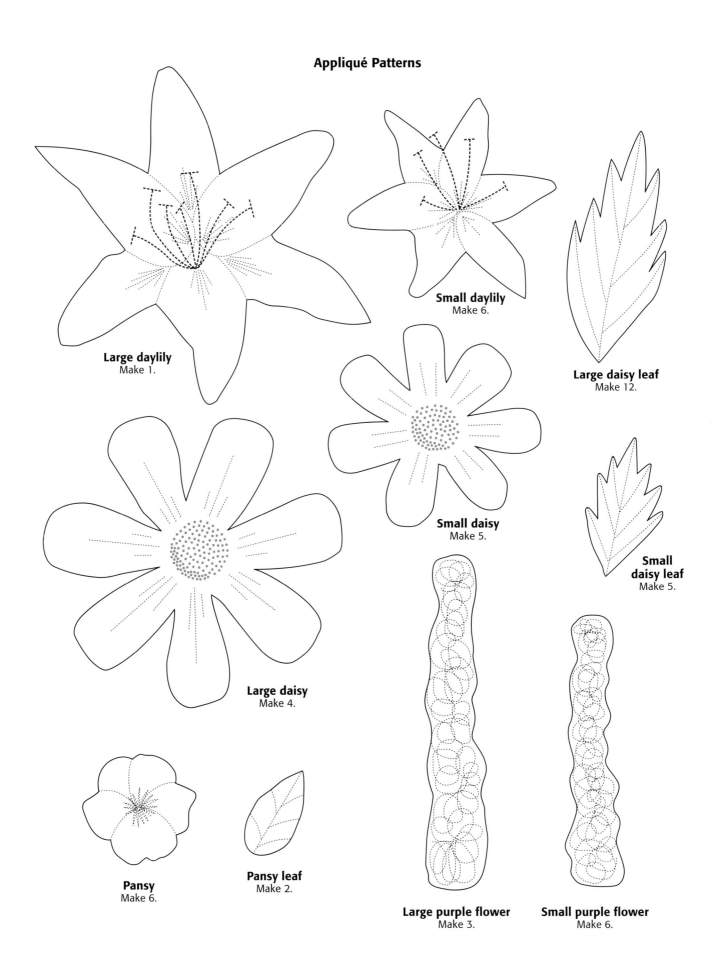

Large daylily
Make 1.

Small daylily
Make 6.

Large daisy leaf
Make 12.

Small daisy
Make 5.

Small daisy leaf
Make 5.

Large daisy
Make 4.

Pansy
Make 6.

Pansy leaf
Make 2.

Large purple flower
Make 3.

Small purple flower
Make 6.

Appliqué Patterns

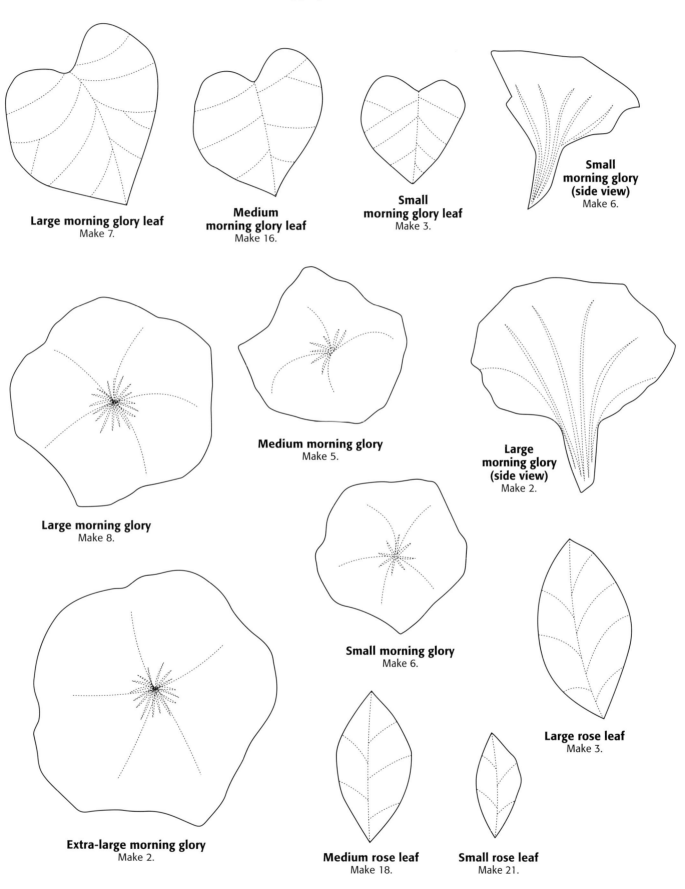

Large morning glory leaf
Make 7.

Medium morning glory leaf
Make 16.

Small morning glory leaf
Make 3.

Small morning glory (side view)
Make 6.

Medium morning glory
Make 5.

Large morning glory (side view)
Make 2.

Large morning glory
Make 8.

Small morning glory
Make 6.

Large rose leaf
Make 3.

Extra-large morning glory
Make 2.

Medium rose leaf
Make 18.

Small rose leaf
Make 21.

CIRCLE PATTERNS

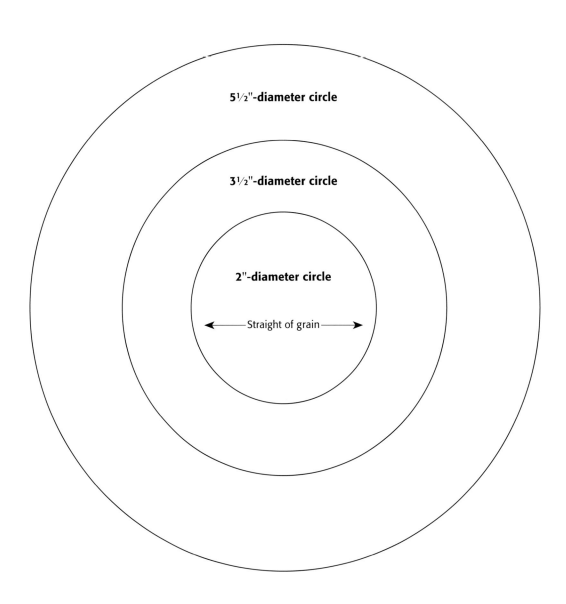

5½"-diameter circle

3½"-diameter circle

2"-diameter circle

←——— Straight of grain ———→

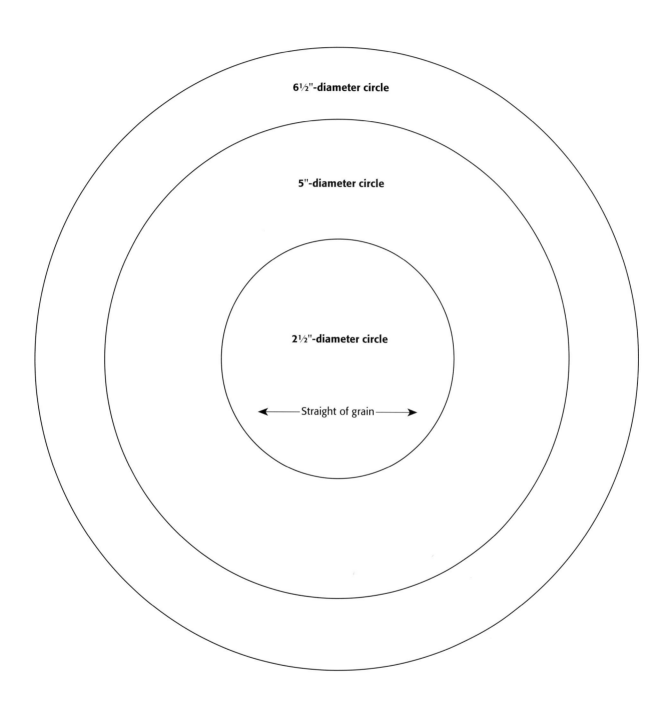

6½"-diameter circle

5"-diameter circle

2½"-diameter circle

←———Straight of grain———→

CIRCLE PATTERNS

ABOUT THE AUTHORS

Ann Frischkorn and Amy Sandrin

Ann Frischkorn and Amy Sandrin are quilt-making partners—and identical twin sisters—who live one thousand miles apart, in Denver and Chicago respectively. Their quilt-making journey began when Ann took a beginner's quilting class with a neighbor and knew, after the first stitch, this was an art form that she would embrace for the rest of her life. Monkey see, monkey do. Because Ann liked it so much, Amy wasn't about to miss out, so Ann taught her the basics during a summer visit, and they have been quilting avidly for the past 13 years.

Even though they live far apart, the modern conveniences of digital cameras and email allow the sisters to bounce ideas, color schemes, and design elements off of each other instantly. Their first quilting book, *Flower Pounding*, was published in 2001. They feel fortunate to have been featured on a segment of HGTV's *Simply Quilts*, hosted by Alex Anderson, which showcased two different sets of quilting twins. They travel the country lecturing and teaching, and, in their spare time, they also write young-adult fiction novels together.